V   narket,
C   l, after
b   r other
n   nerous
p   iter in
r   adings
t

Also by Vincent McDonnell

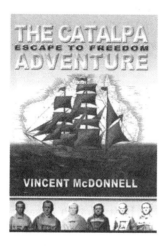

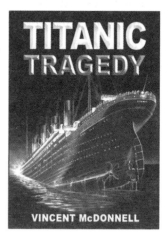

MICHAEL COLLINS
MOST WANTED MAN

Vincent McDonnell

The Collins Press

First published in 2008 by
The Collins Press
West Link Park
Doughcloyne
Wilton
Cork

Reprinted 2012, 2015

A Cataloguing-in-Publication data record is available for this book from the British Library

Paperback ISBN: 978-1-9051-726-27
PDF eBook ISBN: 978-1-8488-906-40
EPUB eBook ISBN: 978-1-8488-992-78
Kindle ISBN: 978-1-8488-992-85

Typesetting by The Collins Press
Typeset in AGaramond 13 pt

Printed in Poland by Drukarnia Skleniarz

Cover images courtesy of the National Library of Ireland.
(L–r): Michael Collins leaving Earlsfort Terrace, Dublin, after the Treaty ratification meeting in 1922; Michael Collins in uniform at Portobello Barracks, Dublin, in 1922.

For my brother Michael, Ann and family

Contents

1

A Daring Escape

One winter morning in 1919, police and British soldiers raided a house in Dublin city. Heavily armed, they came without warning. Their mission was to capture or kill one man. His name was Michael Collins, the most wanted man in the whole of the British Empire.

The house, at 76 Harcourt Street, was Collins' headquarters. From here he planned and directed a guerrilla war against the British Empire. The British government had already made many attempts to capture him, but all had failed. They had even put an enormous price on his head, but so far no one had claimed it.

Now, acting on a tip-off from a spy named Harry Quinlisk, the house was being raided. They hoped that their quarry would be caught off guard and they would at last catch him. By this time Collins had been on the run for over a year, and he knew from his many previous escapes that he had to be vigilant and prepared to flee at any moment.

Now he heard the police vehicles screech to a halt in front of the house. Men shouted urgent orders. There was the thump of heavy boots on the pavement. Michael had to get away.

He was prepared for such an eventuality. The house had a skylight in the roof though which he could escape. He had had a special lightweight ladder made with which he could climb onto the roof. He could then pull the ladder up with him and close the skylight.

Michael was a big man, but urged on by the seriousness of his situation, he scrambled up the ladder with the speed and dexterity of a monkey. He hauled himself out onto the roof and pulled up the ladder behind him. Then he closed the skylight. The shouts and the thumping of the soldiers' boots were louder now. But Michael had no time to wait and listen. He scrambled across the roofs of the adjacent houses until he came to the Standard Hotel which also had a skylight.

He had already arranged that this skylight would be left open permanently for just such an emergency, and that another light ladder would be available so that he could climb down into the hotel.

Michael lowered himself through the skylight, only to discover to his horror that the ladder was missing. He was

A Daring Escape

hanging by his fingertips over the well of the staircase. From here it was a sheer drop to the floor of the hotel lobby far below him. If he fell he would be killed, or at the very least, seriously injured. His only hope was to leap to the safety of the landing. But to reach there he would need to build up momentum to clear the landing rail. Still hanging by his fingertips, he began to swing his body back and forward like a pendulum.

When he felt he had built up sufficient momentum, he released his grip on the edge of the skylight. He leapt into empty space with that sheer drop to the lobby gaping below him. His momentum was sufficient to clear the landing rail, but he caught his foot and fell heavily. His leg was badly injured, but ignoring the pain, he quickly scrambled to his feet. Limping, he descended the stairs to the hotel lobby and made his exit onto the street.

By now a number of his comrades had arrived on the scene. They were watching the entrance to 76 Harcourt Street, which was sealed off by heavily armed soldiers. At any moment the watching men expected to see the man they knew as The Big Fellow being dragged out in handcuffs. Instead, to their utter disbelief, they watched Michael emerge from the Standard Hotel. Apart from the fact that he was limping, he seemed fine. He was smiling, as if at a great joke, calmly hailed a horse-drawn hackney cab and was driven off.

The police, yet again, had failed to catch their most wanted man. After searching No. 76 from top to bottom, they were forced to withdraw empty-handed. Once more Michael Collins had escaped to carry on the fight, a fight he would eventually win.

Within less than two years the British were forced to admit defeat. Collins, with a small group of guerrilla fighters, had beaten the army of the most powerful empire on earth. The British government, unable to capture him or defeat his fighters, was forced to sue for peace.

In October 1921, Michael sat down to negotiate freedom for Ireland with the very government that had sent their policemen and soldiers to capture or kill him. He signed a treaty with the British government that at last gave Ireland her freedom. Less than nine months later he would be dead. For years the British had tried to capture or kill him, but it was to be his, and Ireland's, tragedy that it would be one of his guerrillas, his comrades in the fight for freedom, who would kill him.

This is the story of how Michael Collins, a farmer's son, has come to be regarded as one of the greatest Irishmen of the twentieth century. It is the story of his fight for Irish freedom and of how he defeated the might of the British Empire. It is also the story of how and why he met his death on a lonely road at Béal na mBláth, in his native County Cork, on 22 August 1922.

2

A Boyhood Dream

Michael Collins was born on Thursday 16 October 1890, and named Michael after his father, a farmer who lived at Woodfield, near Clonakilty, County Cork. Michael had five sisters and two brothers and was the youngest of the family. His father was 75 years old when Michael was born, but father and son were very close and spent a great deal of time together on the farm. Because of the relationship that developed between them, for all of his life Michael had a great affection for older people. Michael was a normal boy who loved to play games. With five older sisters and his mother Marianne all doting on him, he never lacked for affection. Though spoiled a little by all the female attention, it nevertheless gave a caring and gentle side to his nature.

During their time together, Michael heard his father relate many stories and legends of Ireland's past, usually of great heroes both real and imaginary. These fired the young boy's interest and imagination. Less than thirty years before Michael's birth, for example, there had been the Fenian rebellion, which failed, and one of the most prominent Fenians had been a local man from Clonakilty, Jeremiah O'Donovan Rossa. He and his fellow Fenians were revered in the area. Here was a real-life local hero for the boy to admire.

Michael also learned of the Great Famine, which had occurred in Ireland in the 1840s. Memories of this terrible famine were still fresh in people's minds. West Cork had been badly affected by it, especially the nearby town of Skibbereen. Here hundreds of victims of the famine – men, women and children – had been buried in mass graves. In sessions of storytelling and song around the Collins' fireside, one of the few entertainments available at that time, Michael heard about these terrible events. His father had lived through the famine, and had seen some of his own neighbours die of hunger and others forced to emigrate.

The cause of the Famine was the land system, whereby English landlords rented land to the Irish at high rents, which the people paid by growing grain crops. To feed themselves, they grew the potato, introduced to Ireland in the seventeenth century. It was easy to grow, even on poor land, and produced a good crop from a small amount of ground. Over time it became the main food source for the majority of Irish peasants. But the potato was prone to a disease known as potato blight, and in the years 1845 to 1847 blight became widespread all over Ireland. As the potato crop failed each year, more than a million people died of hunger or emigrated to Britain or America.

At this time Ireland was ruled directly from London, and had been since 1801. There was no Irish parliament in Dublin. Instead Irish members of parliament (MPs), went to London, where most English MPs did not know much about Ireland. By the time Collins was born, in 1890, there were two main political groups in Ireland. The Irish MPs, the Irish Parliamentary Party, were demanding Home Rule for Ireland. This meant that Ireland would have its own parliament sitting in Dublin, but would still be loyal to the British monarchy. The other group, the Land League, had been founded by Mayoman, Michael Davitt. The aim of the Land League was to rid Ireland of the landlords and their agents and for the Irish to own their own land.

As a young boy, Michael Collins heard much talk about these two groups and their aims. Both wanted to use only peaceful means, but some people believed that those aims could only be achieved by violence. In west Cork some landlords were attacked, their cattle maimed and their crops destroyed. But for the most part, the country was peaceful at this time.

When he was five years old, Michael faced a new challenge. It was time for him to start attending the local school at

Lisavaird. Here he was to meet a man who was to have an enduring influence on his life. Denis Lyons, the headmaster of Lisavaird School, was a strict and severe man but was also fair. He was a strong nationalist who believed that Ireland should have its freedom from England, and that it could only be gained by rebellion. He reinforced Michael's love of Ireland, first kindled by his father.

One other man was to greatly influence Michael during his childhood, James Santry, the local blacksmith. Michael spent a great deal of time at the forge at Lisavaird, a gathering place where the local men met to smoke and talk of local events and to have their horses shod and farm implements made or repaired. Santry was another passionate nationalist. During the rebellions of 1848 and 1867, pikes for the rebels had been forged on the very anvil he was still using. But the pikes had been no match for the guns of the trained English soldiers and the rebellions had failed.

A new campaign against landlords and agents, led by groups like the Land League, gradually made the British government realise that in order to have peace in Ireland, the land would have to be given back to the local farmers. A number of Land Acts were passed. Under these acts, land was purchased from the landlords and given to the farmers. While the Irish tenants were winning their fight, Michael Collins Senior died in 1897, when Michael himself was just six years old. On his deathbed, the father pointed to his youngest son and told the people there to mind this child. One day, he said, he will do great things for Ireland.

Over the next six years Michael grew into a fine strong boy. He helped out on the farm and attended school. But there was time for fun too. He played football and hurling and bowling, which was played on the roads with a heavy metal ball. One threw the ball along the road, and whoever reached a particular point in the least number of throws was declared the winner. Collins was a fine athlete, good at running and jumping. He also excelled at wrestling and was always challenging his friends to a wrestling match. Often he would take on two or three opponents at a time.

There was little work in the west Cork area. A farm would usually pass to the eldest son, and the other children would often emigrate to earn a living. At twelve, therefore, Michael left Lisavaird School and went to live with his sister Margaret in Clonakilty. Here he attended a secondary school to study for the civil service exam. If he passed that he could obtain a job in the Post Office in London, where his sister Hannie was already employed. Margaret was married to P. J. O'Driscoll, who ran a local paper, and Michael wrote for the paper as well as attending school. After three years he sat the civil service exam in Cork city and passed. He was then offered a position as a boy clerk in the Post Office Savings Bank in London.

Michael Collins

At fifteen years of age Michael got his first long trousers. He packed his few possessions into a suitcase and took the train and boat to England, and a new life in London.

3

The Young Rebel

In July 1906 Michael went to live with his sister Hannie in West Kensington, in London. Close by was the Post Office Savings Bank where Hannie worked, and where he began his first job as a junior clerk. Brought up on a remote farm in rural Ireland, he was now living in one of the largest and busiest cities in the world. At that time London was the centre of the most powerful empire on earth.

Hannie did her best to be a steadying influence on her brother, but Michael liked his new-found freedom and being with his friends, especially Seán Hurley, with whom he'd grown up. His love of sport continued, and he became a member of the Geraldines GAA club. He played football and hurling, and won numerous medals. He wasn't a skilful player but his strength, enthusiasm and determination to win made him a very powerful opponent. He also developed his love for athletics and here again he won many medals. He was a fine athlete, especially in events where power and strength were required. He was an exceptional sprinter and excelled at the long jump.

His determination and desire to win at all costs often got him into trouble. If a row broke out over a disputed score, Michael would be found in the middle of it. In those situations there were no rules and often Michael would use unsporting means to win. He loved wrestling and here again would resort to unsporting means if he felt he was losing. One such act was known as 'having a bit of ear'. If in danger of losing, he would bite an opponent's ear until it bled, thus forcing him to give up. After such a bloody encounter there were many that wished they hadn't picked a fight with him. Soon it became known that Mick Collins was not a man to be crossed.

Under Hannie's influence, he developed a love for the theatre and regularly attended the latest plays. He also read widely, not just English writers but Irish writers who had nationalist leanings. He joined the Gaelic League, which promoted Irish language and culture, and took Irish language lessons. He also attended night classes to improve his education. He met a young woman named Susan Killeen from County Clare, his first girlfriend. They regularly went dancing and to the theatre.

In 1907 Michael suffered a terrible blow when his mother died of cancer. He was just seventeen and now had lost both parents. He was far from home and even though he had Hannie's support, he felt the loss greatly. As a balm for his grief, he threw himself more wholeheartedly into sport. He got involved in the organisation of the Geraldines club and became its treasurer. During his time in London he also acted as treasurer for the London GAA. The experience he gained in these positions was to stand him in good stead later.

Michael left the Post Office to work in a firm of stockbrokers. Later he joined the Board of Trade as a clerk. His last job in London was with the Guaranty Trust Company of New York, where he worked until January 1916.

One of his most important friends was Sam Maguire from Dunmanway, not far from Woodfield, a Protestant nationalist. Today he is best remembered for the Sam Maguire Cup, which is presented in Croke Park to the winning captain of the All-Ireland senior football champions.

In November 1909, at Barnsbury Hall in Islington, Michael Collins was sworn in as a member of the Irish Republican Brotherhood (IRB) by Sam Maguire, and later became its treasurer. The IRB had been founded as a secret society by James Stephens in 1858, and was closely associated with the Fenians. Men like Stephens and O'Donovan Rossa had belonged to both groups. While the Fenian rising of 1867 failed, its ideals lived on in the IRB, whose members continued to believe in rebellion as the only means of gaining freedom for Ireland. At the time that

Michael joined, the IRB had been in decline. But all that was soon to change.

In 1905 Arthur Griffith, a journalist, had founded a new Irish political party, Sinn Féin. Griffith believed that Ireland could gain her freedom through non-violent means. He suggested that Irish MPs should not attend the parliament in London but should set up a parliament in Dublin. In their first election, Sinn Féin failed completely, but it would later play a major part in Ireland's fight for freedom.

There was still hope that Ireland would be granted Home Rule. This hope increased in 1910, because the MPs of the Irish Parliamentary Party now held the balance of power in the London parliament. Their leader, John Redmond, demanded Home Rule, and Herbert Asquith, the leader of the Liberal Party which was in power, agreed to introduce a Home Rule Bill in return for their support. This bill, granting Home Rule to Ireland, passed through the British parliament in 1912.

Not everyone in Ireland was happy with this state of affairs. A number of counties in Ulster, where the population was mostly Protestant, did not wish to be separated from Britain, and did not want to be a minority in a Catholic-dominated Ireland. Edward Carson, a lawyer, organised Ulster's opposition to Home Rule, along with James Craig, a wealthy, northern businessman.

Before the Home Rule Bill was passed, Craig organised a gathering of 50,000 supporters at his home town, Craigavon, near Belfast in 1911. Following this, still larger protests were organised. It was men from these protests who formed the Ulster Volunteer Force (UVF), founded in 1913 by Carson to defend Ulster from Home Rule. It numbered around 100,000 men who were determined to fight if necessary. Carson also threatened to set up a separate parliament in Belfast if Home Rule was introduced. A huge shipment of arms was imported from Germany for the UVF. The police knew of this illegal shipment, but did nothing to stop it. Now Carson commanded a formidable armed force.

In response to the founding of the UVF, an Irish nationalist, Eoin MacNeill, founded the Irish Volunteers in Dublin in November 1913. His intention was to defend Home Rule when it was eventually introduced. In London, a branch of the Irish Volunteers was formed, and Michael Collins was sworn in as a member by Seán Hurley in April 1914. Each week, he and Seán drilled with their fellow Volunteers.

Guns were required to arm the Volunteers. Roger Casement and Erskine Childers went to Germany for rifles and ammunition, and in July 1914 Childers sailed his yacht, *Asgard*, into Howth, County Dublin, with the arms on board. As the army and police tried to intercept them on their way into Dublin, a crowd that had gathered prevented them. The soldiers opened fire, killing three innocent citizens and injuring several more. These actions made it clear to many of the Irish Volunteers where

Britain's loyalties really lay – not with the Irish Volunteers, who supported Home Rule, but with the Ulster Volunteers who opposed it.

Unknown to MacNeill, many of the Volunteers did not agree with his intention of defending Home Rule. They believed that the Volunteers should be used to rebel openly against Britain and obtain Irish freedom by force of arms. Among these men were Thomas Clarke, an old Fenian, Patrick Pearse and Seán MacDermott. They were members of the IRB and were secretly planning rebellion. All they needed was the right opportunity to put their plan into action.

In August 1914, the First World War began in Europe. Britain found itself at war with Germany. If Home Rule was introduced in Ireland, it would almost certainly lead to a bloody conflict there, while Britain was fighting in Europe, so the Home Rule Act was suspended until the end of the War.

John Redmond reluctantly accepted this decision, and urged the Irish Volunteers to go and fight with Britain in defence of small European countries like Belgium. This caused a split, and those who sided with Redmond became known as the National Volunteers. Many of them did join the British army, and went to fight in France. The remaining Irish Volunteers thought that it wasn't right that Irishmen should go and fight for freedom for small nations while Ireland itself was not free, and saw the War as the opportunity they had been waiting for. They knew that their numbers were few and that they were unlikely to succeed, but they believed that a rebellion was necessary to rouse the people of Ireland, who seemed happy to accept the promise of Home Rule when the War ended.

Michael Collins saw this as his opportunity to fight for Ireland. He would fight like those heroes of the past that he had heard about when he was a boy. As a member of the IRB and the Irish Volunteers in London, he knew that a rebellion was being planned. He was determined that he would be there to fight.

He had been considering going to join his brother, Patrick, in Chicago but he now decided to head for Dublin, and left his job in the Guaranty Trust. When he told them he was going to enlist, they thought that he meant the British army, and gave him a bonus. It has been suggested that he left England just to avoid conscription, a compulsory call-up to the British army for all young men, but Michael was going to join his fellow Volunteers in Dublin to fight for Ireland.

4

Easter Rising

The Irish Volunteers numbered about 15,000 members, supported by about 700 members of a women's auxiliary, Cumann na mBan. The soldiers were poorly armed but made up for this in their passionate belief in their cause. The leaders were aware that the British army, with its highly trained professional soldiers, would be much too powerful for a small number of poorly trained and poorly armed rebels, even though it was badly stretched by the fighting in Europe. They knew too that if the Rising failed, they would be executed as traitors. But they believed that a blood sacrifice was necessary to stir the patriotic fervour of the Irish people. Among those who knew they were almost certainly going to their deaths were the leaders Patrick Pearse, Joseph Plunkett, Thomas Clarke, Thomas MacDonagh, Éamonn Ceannt, Seán MacDermott and James Connolly.

Easter Rising

When Michael Collins arrived back in Dublin, he took a part-time job working on the accounts of the Plunkett family who lived at Larkfield, in South Dublin. Their son Joseph was one of the planners of the rebellion. In the grounds of the estate were living a group of men who had left England to escape conscription, and were training for the fight. He also took a job with Craig Gardner, an accountancy firm. He kept in close contact with Clarke and MacDermott, members of the secret Military Council of the IRB, and met many others who would take part in the Rising, such as Cathal Brugha and Harry Boland.

Collins was appointed a Captain in the Irish Volunteers. Such was their perilous monetary situation that he had to buy his own uniform. He then became an assistant (aide de camp) to Joseph Plunkett, who was ill with tuberculosis.

A date was set for the Rising – Easter Sunday, 23 April. The plan was for the Volunteers to take over a number of strategic positions in Dublin city, such as the Four Courts, Jacob's Biscuit Factory, Boland's Mill, the South Dublin Union Workhouse and Liberty Hall. Their headquarters would be the General Post Office (GPO) in O'Connell Street (then called Sackville Street). In the Rising, the Irish Volunteers would be joined by the much smaller Irish Citizen Army (ICA), led by James Connolly.

This army had been formed in 1913, when a trade union leader, James Larkin, had organised a strike in Dublin for better pay and conditions for workers. Connolly, a Scottish socialist, had supported Larkin. The police, who were on the side of the employers, used violence against the strikers. It was to protect the strikers from such brutality that Connolly had formed the ICA. The strikers lost and eventually had to return to work, but the ICA remained intact and now joined with the rebels.

Roger Casement went again to Germany to try and obtain more arms, and was promised a shipment of some 20,000 rifles, as the Volunteers outside of Dublin were poorly armed. These were sent to Ireland in a ship called the *Aud*, while Casement returned to Ireland in a German submarine. But British spies had learned of the shipment and Casement's involvement and were lying in wait.

Casement and the arms were to be landed at Banna Strand on the coast of County Kerry. On Good Friday morning, Casement landed at Banna and was immediately arrested. (He was later tried for treason, convicted and hanged in London.) As the *Aud*, with its cargo of arms, approached the Irish coast, the Royal Navy was lying in wait. The German crew refused to surrender the vessel and scuttled it, sinking it to the bottom of the sea. The valuable cargo of rifles, so desperately needed, was lost.

This was a terrible blow to the leaders. They now could not arm Volunteers in places like Limerick and Cork. It had been hoped that there would be risings in other parts of the country and not just in Dublin. If the Rising was to have any hope of success it was essential that there be a countrywide rebellion.

This was not the only problem the leaders encountered. Because of the need for secrecy there was no public knowledge of the proposed Rising. The orders merely stated that the Volunteers would meet for manoeuvres on Easter Sunday, something they did regularly. Most of them did not even know that they would be taking part in an actual rising. When MacNeill finally learned of the proposal, he was horrified and immediately issued an order forbidding it. This caused great confusion among the Volunteers, not helped by the fact that communications were poor at the time.

The British authorities had also learned of the proposed Rising. They had intended arresting the leaders, but when Casement was captured and the *Aud* scuttled, they assumed that the Rising would not now go ahead. MacNeill's order forbidding a Rising also reassured them that all was well. But the leaders decided to go ahead with their plans, even though it was certain that the Rising would fail. Orders were issued that the manoeuvres planned for Easter Sunday would now instead take place on Easter Monday, 24 April.

In preparation for this, Joseph Plunkett, just out of hospital where he had had an operation, moved into the Metropole Hotel in Sackville Street on Saturday, accompanied by Captain Michael Collins. It was a frantic weekend as orders and counter-orders went back and forth. As Plunkett was Director of Military Operations, Collins was at the forefront of organising and dealing with all these confusing orders.

On Easter Monday morning, under the eyes of British army officers, Michael Collins helped Joseph Plunkett from the Metropole Hotel. By car, Collins and Plunkett travelled to Liberty Hall, the headquarters of Connolly's trade union movement. From here, led by Connolly, Pearse and Clarke, they marched to the GPO. Other groups of Volunteers hurried off to take up their positions, while the Irish Citizen Army set off for St Stephen's Green. The men who had been camping in the grounds at Larkfield now made their way into the city to take part in the Rising. They had to commandeer a tram to take them in and George Plunkett, Joseph's father, who was with them, insisted on paying their fares! There were little more than a thousand men altogether, due to all the confusion.

This was to be Michael Collins' first experience of rebellion. Just like many of the rebellions he had heard of in his childhood, it was to be a mixture of romanticism, bravery, sacrifice, death and foolishness. It was to end in apparent failure, but ultimately was to succeed in its aims of rousing the Irish people.

Though it was Easter Monday morning, the GPO was open for business. Those in the building were ordered out, except for a British officer who was taken prisoner. The general public were puzzled by all this activity, but were amused too. They thought it was a joke.

The Volunteers now set up barricades, broke out the windows and prepared positions from which they could fire on any attackers. Provisions of food and water were obtained from the Metropole Hotel. Collins emptied barrels of porter down the drains – he was determined that the Volunteers were not going to get drunk. Meanwhile, the leaders gathered on the steps of the GPO. To a bemused group of Dubliners, who had gathered to see what was happening, Patrick Pearse read out what became known as The Proclamation. They declared that Ireland was now a republic and that they were willing to fight and die for it.

On the roof of the GPO, the Irish flag was raised. It fluttered in the breeze, a visual declaration that the Republic of Ireland now existed, at least in the minds of the Volunteers. But instead of instilling the crowd that had gathered with patriotic fervour, it only made them laugh. They heckled and taunted the Volunteers. However, as news of the Rising spread among the ordinary people, their mood turned to anger.

The poorer classes in Dublin lived in appalling conditions in what were known as tenements, tall narrow buildings without proper heating, light or sanitation.

Whole families, sometimes a dozen or more persons, lived in one room. This helped to spread disease, which killed thousands every year. There was little work available, but this situation had changed in 1914. With the outbreak of war, soldiers were needed for the British army, and many men from these poor families had joined up. Now they were in France or Belgium fighting for Britain against the Germans. While they were in the army, their families back in Dublin received 'separation money', which provided food for the wives and children.

These poor people, mostly women, now saw that the Volunteers were fighting the very country that paid the vital 'separation money'. If they didn't get that money, they and their children would go hungry. Rather than supporting the Volunteers, these people bitterly opposed them. They saw them, not as patriots, but as thugs and blackguards. Many made their way to the GPO to taunt the Volunteers while others just laughed, still enjoying the joke. But it was no joke, as they were soon to find out when a troop of mounted lancers charged down Sackville Street. The Volunteers in the GPO opened fire. Horses and men fell in the street under a hail of bullets. The crowd withdrew in panic, at least for the moment.

Throughout the city, the Volunteers seized the strategic buildings which had been chosen at the planning stage. Dublin Castle, the centre of British rule in Ireland, was also attacked, but the Volunteers did not press home their attack, thinking that it would be impossible to take the building. In fact the castle was poorly defended and could have been taken. It was a missed opportunity.

In the GPO, under the guidance of Connolly, the Volunteers prepared for the coming fight. In case they had to leave in a hurry, they broke through the walls at the rear so that they could retreat into the houses in Moore Street. They tunnelled from house to house, prepared to fight street by street if necessary.

In Dublin Castle the authorities were taken by surprise. Because it was a bank holiday, many army officers and Castle officials had gone to the races at Fairyhouse. Reinforcements were needed, and these were brought in from the Curragh camp in County Kildare. Other reinforcements were ordered from England, and more artillery was obtained. The British plan was to encircle the Volunteers and then close in, trapping them. However, they had to wait for the reinforcements and the artillery, so over the first few days there was little fighting in the city.

Widespread looting broke out when the citizens became aware that there was no law and order. Fires broke out in the houses near the GPO, started by the looters. Flames lit up the night sky. For those in the GPO, a sense of unreality set in. They had seized the building, declared an Irish Republic and now there was a stalemate. Collins observed what was happening and realised that the Rising was doomed to failure. The Volunteers were too few in number, too poorly armed and organised. They could not fight the might of the British Empire this way. He saw also that men like Pearse and MacDonagh were dreamers. They had a romantic view of Ireland and of how she might win her freedom. Collins, ever practical, realised that she would have to win it some other way.

By Thursday, the British were in a position to attack the GPO. A gunboat, the *Helga*, sailed up the Liffey and took up position. With a salvo of shells, the fighting began. The GPO was bombarded. Shells smashed into the building while the walls were riddled with bullets. Soon the roof caught fire. Before long, many of the buildings in Sackville Street were ablaze. Connolly had earlier led a group of Volunteers outside the GPO, but they came under heavy machine-gun fire and bullets shattered Connolly's thighbone. In terrible agony, he was dragged back to the GPO. His injuries only added to the sense of doom among the Volunteers.

By now many were dead or injured. The building was burning fiercely. The situation was hopeless, and there was no alternative but to withdraw. The Volunteers, taking the injured Connolly with them, left the GPO through the holes in the rear wall, and headed across Moore Street under heavy fire. They took shelter in the houses on Moore Street, but were trapped, and could go no further.

They had already held out for longer than any of them could have expected. To continue fighting on would mean certain death for a great many more Volunteers. Reluctantly the leaders decided to surrender. A truce was arranged and on Saturday afternoon, 29 April, Pearse and his Volunteers surrendered, as did other groups of Volunteers around the city. They were tired and dispirited. Their uniforms, worn with such pride and hope and promise on Easter Monday morning, were now tattered and stained with ash and dust and blood.

On Sackville Street a terrible sight greeted them. Dublin was still ablaze. Burnt-out and shelled buildings stood roofless and windowless against the smoke and flames. The street was littered with dead bodies and was slick with blood. One of the dead was a famous Volunteer known as The O'Rahilly. Now his body lay riddled with bullets. Close by was the burnt-out skeleton of his beloved de Dion motor car. But Collins had a much more personal blow to bear. His great childhood friend, Seán Hurley, who had been with him during his years in London, was dead. This was the first close friend Michael lost in the fight for Irish freedom. Over the coming years he would lose many more friends, but that first one cut deeply.

Hungry, tired and depressed by the killing and the failure of the Rising, the Volunteers were marched up Sackville Street and on to the Rotunda Hospital. They were a bedraggled group, demoralised and uncertain of their fate. No one who saw them could have foreseen then that they had in their actions ignited a fire in Ireland that would eventually lead to Ireland gaining her independence six years later.

5

Prisoner

The surrendered Volunteers were held in front of the Rotunda Hospital. They were tired, hungry and dispirited, and many were wounded. They were packed tight into the small area, surrounded by armed British soldiers. One British officer, Captain Lee Wilson, strode up and down among the prisoners, striking them. A cruel, sadistic man, he forced some of the prisoners to stand on the steps of the Rotunda and strip naked. One man humiliated in this way was Tom Clarke, who had an injured arm and had difficulty using it. Enraged by Clarke's inability to undress quickly, Lee Wilson tore off his clothes. This caused the wound in Clarke's arm to bleed, adding to his misery.

Even though it was the end of April, it was bitterly cold. For an old man like Clarke, who had spent so much of his life in

English jails, this was not only a public humiliation but also a physical ordeal. Collins, who admired Clarke, protested at this treatment, as did others, but they were beaten and kicked until they were silent. Michael would almost certainly have physically attacked Lee Wilson, but was prevented from doing so by his colleagues. They cautioned him to wait – their day would eventually come. For now he had to stand helplessly by and watch his old friend and comrade humiliated. He silently vowed that one day he would see that Lee Wilson was punished. Years later, on a lonely road in County Wexford, Lee Wilson was shot dead. Collins did not see the killing as revenge but simply as justice for Tom Clarke.

The next day the prisoners were marched to Richmond Barracks. There, plain-clothes detectives known as G-men (members of G Division of the police) picked out the leaders for court martial and certain execution. A G-man who was present that day was Joe Kavanagh. He went among the prisoners asking if they wanted anything or if he could do anything for them. He also offered to take messages to their loved ones. Naturally, the prisoners were suspicious of him and refused to speak to him, but he was in earnest. Later he would play a major part in the life of Michael Collins.

Because Collins had only come from London the previous January, the G-men had little information on him. As the G-men completed their selection, they were unaware that they were making a terrible mistake by ignoring him. For some of them, like Detective Daniel Hoey, who at the last minute identified Seán MacDermott, thus sending him to his execution, the mistake was to cost them their lives. Some years later Michael Collins would have Hoey and many of his colleagues shot.

While the leaders were taken off to prison, the remaining prisoners were again marched through the city to the cattle boat that would take them to prison. On the journey the citizens of Dublin came out to watch. Some cheered and shouted encouragement, but others hissed and spat at the prisoners, angered by their actions. These people had seen their city shelled and burned, and 300 citizens had been killed in the fighting.

At the port, the prisoners were loaded onto a cattle boat bound for England. There they were taken to Stafford Detention Centre and held in solitary confinement. It was Collins' first taste of prison and he loathed it. He was a man who loved sport and physical activity, and the company of his fellow men.

At first Michael had no contact with the outside world. But as he was later to do in many other circumstances, he set up his own communications, using the friendliest of his jailers after winning their grudging respect. It was a gift he had and one that would later prove invaluable – this ability to gain the confidence of friend and enemy alike. In Stafford, Michael took the first steps in his new life as the leader of Ireland's fight for freedom.

Prisoner

When the prisoners were eventually allowed to meet, he began to exert his influence. He was usually at the centre of any physical activity and soon his fellow prisoners began to exploit his quick temper. They would rile him until he became enraged, fight him in rough and tumble and then laugh with him. They thought it a great joke but for Michael it was a way of letting off steam. But there was a gentler, quieter side to Collins. In Stafford he read books and studied and wrote letters to friends, including Susan Killeen.

Unknown to the prisoners, events were occurring in Ireland which would change the course of Irish history. The leaders of the rebellion were tried by court martial and found guilty of rebellion. Over a period of weeks they were executed at Kilmainham Jail and were buried within the prison walls. Joseph Plunkett married Grace Gifford in his prison cell. She spent ten minutes with him, and he was shot the next morning. As each execution was announced, public outrage grew, fanned by stories like that of Plunkett's wedding. It reached its peak with the news of James Connolly's execution. Suffering terrible pain from his leg wound and unable to stand, he was strapped in a chair and shot.

This outrage was not confined to Ireland. Worldwide attention was now focused on the country, and even in Britain, the executions were condemned. The government ordered a halt to further executions, and the remaining condemned men were sentenced to prison instead. One of these was Éamon de Valera, now the only surviving Commandant. He may have been spared because he was an American citizen.

News of the executions eventually reached the prisoners in Stafford. Collins was devastated; Clarke, MacDermott and Plunkett had not only been his comrades but his friends as well. He knew that they had died as they wished, making the blood sacrifice that Pearse thought necessary. But did they have to die? It was a question Michael would ask himself again and again during his time as a prisoner. Later he would see that the deaths had achieved what the leaders had wanted to achieve. They had woken the Irish people from their apathy. They had shown them in stark reality the injustice of British rule in Ireland.

6

The Big Fellow

The prisoners were moved to Frongoch internment camp. It was still a prison, but it felt like freedom when compared to the bleak prison at Stafford the Volunteers had just left. Frongoch was in the Welsh countryside, which with its rolling green hills so resembled the Irish countryside. The camp, once an old distillery, was divided into two sections. In the south section were the distillery buildings. The north section consisted of huts in which the men lived. There were other facilities like a cookhouse, a hospital, and a barber's as well as workshops.

Collins was sent to a hut in the north camp, which could sleep thirty men. Here almost immediately he began to exert his presence. Soon his hut was the scene of horseplay and regular wrestling matches, where two or even three men would take on Michael. He had a fierce temper, which often got the better of him. When that happened, he would 'have a bit of ear'. Wrestling was something he would also indulge in later during his years on the run, usually leaving his hapless opponent with his ears streaming blood.

Whatever furniture was in the hut was often smashed. Bunks were upturned and blankets strewn about the floor. Feathers swirled in the air like snowflakes as pillows burst in the regular pillow fights. Those who valued their safely usually kept out of the way while three or four large men fought in the relatively confined space. Michael's hut was known as the noisiest in the camp and possibly the most dangerous for the inmates. But to the men, the wrestling matches were a way of dealing with the boredom of prison. Always the sportsman, Michael helped to organise sports where again he excelled. He was a poor loser and would use any ploy to win. This did not endear him to some of the prisoners and there were many who disliked him.

But it was not all fun and games. He read a great deal, studied, and wrote many letters. He made friends with the guards and used them to communicate with the other men in the camp and with the outside world. It was in Frongoch that those who had been members of the IRB began to meet again.

At the time of the Rising, the leadership of the IRB had mostly consisted of older men. Now younger men like Michael Collins began to exert their influence. Like Collins, they were well aware of the failures of the Rising. They realised that if they were going to fight again, they must not make the same mistakes. The older men of the IRB were pushed aside. The new war, when it began, would be a very different kind of war. This would be a war of secrecy, of hit and run, of men who struck at the enemy and then melted away in the darkness like ghosts.

Many men were envious of Michael Collins – they thought he was too big for his boots. They gave him a nickname, The Big Fellow, because they thought he was big-headed, a show-off and a man who used his strength unfairly. However, the term 'Big Fellow' was later to become one of affection and admiration.

While Frongoch had many advantages over a prison, it was not a very pleasant place. The weather was often wet and cold, even in the summer. Conditions in the camp were perfect for vermin, and rats proved to be a constant nuisance for the inmates and authorities alike.

A more pressing worry was the threat of conscription. Though conscription still did not apply to men who had lived in Ireland, it did apply to those, like Michael Collins, who had been living in Britain. A campaign against conscription was organised. One of Collins' suggestions was that the men should refuse to answer their names at roll call so that they could not be identified. Prisoners also refused to work in the local quarries or mend the roads.

The authorities reacted by refusing to deliver letters and parcels. The leaders and worst troublemakers were sent to the south camp. Collins joined them there. Here again he managed to set up communications with the other sections of the camp and somehow managed to obtain cigarettes for the men. This helped him to cement friendships which would later prove invaluable to him.

Conditions at the camp deteriorated. Men who continued to refuse to co-operate were placed in solitary confinement. Food was poor at the best of times; now many became ill through confinement and inadequate nutrition, and doctors were not allowed to treat them. The general public gradually became aware of the conditions in Frongoch, and there were protests in Ireland, Britain and America. When a large number of prisoners went on hunger strike, British MPs added their voices to the protests. Eventually the government was forced to take action and began to release the prisoners. Just before Christmas 1916, Michael Collins was released.

He returned to Dublin on Christmas morning and, along with another Frongoch prisoner and west Cork man, Gearóid O'Sullivan, called to see their friend, Joe O'Reilly from Bantry. He had known Michael in London and had been a prisoner with him in Stafford and Frongoch. O'Reilly shared a room with another man and both were in bed when the two returning internees burst in. They dragged O'Reilly out of bed and wrestled him. Collins bit him on both ears until they bled. For O'Reilly's roommate it was a terrifying experience, but for

O'Reilly himself it was simply Collins having a bit of fun.

Later Joe O'Reilly would become one of Michael's closest friends, his loyal ally and helper, his messenger boy, the man on whom Michael would continually vent his anger and frustration. O'Reilly never wavered in his loyalty to his leader.

Collins and O'Sullivan went off to celebrate their new-found freedom. That evening Michael took the train from Dublin and returned to his beloved west Cork, arriving at Woodfield to learn that his grandmother had just died. He stayed in west Cork for a few weeks before returning to Dublin. He knew that it was in Dublin he could best achieve his boyhood dream of winning Ireland her freedom.

7

Preparing for War

When Michael Collins arrived in Dublin in January 1917, he was unemployed. As a rebel and a prisoner, he was not a suitable candidate for employment. The Rising had caused great inconvenience and loss of income for businessmen, and they were not kindly disposed to those they held responsible.

Many of the Volunteers and their families were living in desperate poverty. In order to help them an organisation had been set up, called the Irish National Aid and Volunteer Dependants' Fund. It raised funds wherever it could, much of its money coming from supporters in America. Collins applied for the job of secretary, and was recommended for it by Kathleen Clarke, Tom's widow. With his skills in bookkeeping and accounts, he was an excellent secretary. Those who came to him for help were met with sympathy, though he could be gruff in manner. Even his enemies had to admit to his kindness and understanding of those who were desperate. He checked every claim carefully, and was often seen cycling about the city making sure that claims were genuine.

In this job he again came into contact with many of the Volunteers, and formed new friendships or renewed old ones. One of the most important of these friendships was with Harry Boland, a tailor. With men like Boland, he helped to reorganise the IRB and the Volunteers. Collins became a member of the Supreme Council of the IRB, and here, with like-minded men, he began to plan a new and very different war against Britain.

However, many of the older IRB men and Volunteers disliked and distrusted Collins, particularly Cathal Brugha. Brugha had been seriously wounded in 1916, but had refused to surrender. It was thought that he would die of his wounds, but he survived. He disliked secret organisations and was opposed to the IRB. He also believed in openly fighting the enemy, as he had in 1916. With such views, it was inevitable that he and Collins would disagree.

Those who had not taken part in the Rising still supported the idea of Home Rule, but already the British were promising the Unionists in Ulster, led by Carson, that they could have their own parliament in Belfast. Collins and others like him did not want Home Rule. They wanted a free, 32-county Ireland, including

Ulster. They supported Sinn Féin, the party founded by Arthur Griffith, who also believed in a free, 32-county republic, but Griffith wished to achieve this through peaceful means.

In February 1917, a by-election was held in County Roscommon. George Plunkett, father of the executed Joseph, stood for Sinn Féin and was elected. Agreeing with Sinn Féin policy, called 'abstention', he refused to take his seat in the London parliament. In May 1917 another by-election was held, in County Longford. Collins worked for the Sinn Féin candidate, Joseph McGuinness, who was still in prison. McGuinness won, which was another great victory for Sinn Féin. However Michael's involvement in the Longford election was to have another great significance for him. It was here that he first met a woman named Kitty Kiernan, and fell in love with her. Unfortunately, Harry Boland was also interested in her.

Around this time the British released most of the remaining prisoners. Among them was Éamon de Valera, who had won a by-election in West Clare. The Volunteers regarded him as their rightful leader, assuming that he still believed in achieving Irish freedom through violence. But de Valera no longer believed in violence and, like Cathal Brugha, despised secret organisations like the IRB. Conflict with Michael Collins was inevitable.

The British government, alarmed by the election successes of Sinn Féin and by speeches and demonstrations supporting those they saw as rebels, acted harshly. Many men were arrested, court-martialled and sentenced to prison, among them Austin Stack and Thomas Ashe, both friends of Michael Collins. In prison they were treated as common criminals. Seeking to change this, they and other prisoners went on hunger strike in September 1917. After five days, the authorities force-fed the prisoners, causing the death of Thomas Ashe.

Ashe was young and handsome. He had been arrested simply for making speeches. His death at such a young age, and in such circumstances, shocked the people of the country. It also devastated Michael Collins. He was laid out in his Volunteer uniform, and more than 30,000 people came to pay their respects. Massive crowds attended his funeral, where Volunteers marched openly in their uniforms. At the graveside a volley of shots was fired.

Michael Collins gave the funeral speech. Afterwards he wept at the death of his friend. Ashe's death displayed the growing strength of the Volunteers, and the fact that Collins gave the graveside oration showed how important a figure he was now becoming in the IRB. He was also an asset to Sinn Féin in the elections with his undoubted charm and ability to impress a crowd with his words. But Sinn Féin and the IRB had very different objectives. Griffith wanted Ireland to have its own parliament in Dublin, through peaceful means. On the other hand, the IRB wanted an Irish Republic. They were aware that

Britain would never willingly concede this. If the IRB wanted it, they would have to fight for it.

Éamon de Valera was also gaining prominence. As an elected member of Sinn Féin, he felt that he should be its leader. Both the Volunteers and the IRB supported him, so Griffith, not wishing to cause a split, stood down as leader. With IRB support, de Valera was also chosen as the President of the Volunteers. Michael Collins became Director of Organisation, and other IRB men were also given prominent positions. The Volunteers were now controlled almost completely by IRB men, except for the Chief of Staff, Cathal Brugha.

As Director of Organisation, Collins now began putting his own ideas into practice. Around the country, Volunteers were formed into what were to become known as 'flying columns', groups of local Volunteers who came together to drill. Their intention was to fight a guerrilla war. They would not engage the British army in open battle. Instead, they would strike suddenly and without warning, and then melt back into the countryside to await another opportunity.

Collins travelled round the country to meet them. They were still poorly armed and he tried to obtain arms for them. These were bought or stolen in Britain and smuggled into Ireland, many by sympathisers to the cause. These were people who worked on ships sailing from Britain to Ireland, or on the docks or the railways. Despite the terrible dangers involved, these people helped to bring the arms into Ireland. Now the Volunteers had some of the guns they needed for their coming war. Another source of arms was the police force. If the arms kept at police stations could be stolen, the Volunteers could use them against the enemy. Soon they would be ready to fight this new war.

8

A Network of Spies

At the beginning of 1918 Sinn Féin lost two by-elections. One of them, in Waterford, was to fill the seat left vacant by the death of John Redmond. He had dreamed of obtaining Home Rule for Ireland by peaceful means, but had failed. He died a broken and disillusioned man, his dream in tatters. If it had not been for the First World War, he might have achieved his dream and prevented the violence he had been so anxious to avoid. At the time of his death, his Irish Parliamentary Party was the most important party in Ireland. But all that was soon to change.

Collins began to get help from a number of men who would prove invaluable in the coming war. Some came from the G-men, the plainclothes detectives whose aims were to destroy Michael and men like him. One of these was Joe Kavanagh. He, like most of his colleagues, was an Irishman and had witnessed the failure of British rule in Ireland. He had also seen the different attitude taken by the British government in their dealings with the loyalists in the north. He had sympathy for Sinn Féin, and for what they were trying to achieve, and wanted to help them. His offer of help was at first refused, but then Collins decided to see if it was genuine. Meeting Kavanagh, Michael realised that Kavanagh was genuine in his wish to help. David Neligan and Éamonn Broy (known as Ned), two more G-men, also offered help.

Collins now had access to secret information the British authorities had on himself, the Volunteers, the IRB and Sinn Féin. More important still, he now had access to any plans the British might draw up to deal with him – he could stay one step ahead of the police. Later, when he was on the run, this information was to save him from arrest on many occasions. But most important of all, he was now able to identify other G-men. He obtained details of their lives and of where they lived and when they were most vulnerable.

Joe Kavanagh died a year after meeting Michael Collins, but before he died he introduced to him a new detective, James McNamara. McNamara was one of the most trusted of all the G-men and the information he provided was to prove priceless. Many other members of the police saw the injustice of British rule. Later, when Michael was on the run, many of them would greet him on the street or else turn away and pretend they hadn't seen him.

Collins slowly put together a network of people who were willing to help him. Railway workers and those who worked on the trams, barmen and hotel staff and tradesmen and shop workers, carried messages or passed on information. One who took great risks was Michael's own cousin, Nancy O'Brien. She was in charge of coded messages at Dublin Castle and so was able to smuggle these out. Once she travelled on the train to Cork, carrying a suitcase of arms for her cousin. Because the case was heavy a British officer helped her carry it. Had he been aware of what was in the case she would certainly have been arrested and sent to prison. Without the assistance of these courageous men and women, the campaign Collins was planning might have met with failure.

Two other women were prominent in passing on information. These two women could not have been more different, nor recruited as 'spies' in such different ways. Lily Mernin worked at Dublin Castle and was related to another Volunteer. She knew many of the G-men by sight and was able to identify them. The other woman was Josephine Marchmont. She worked in the military barracks in Cork city and came from a family that had served the British Empire with great distinction.

Josephine had two young sons. Their father had been killed in the First World War, and their grandmother had taken the children to live with her in Wales and would not let Josephine have them back. On Michael's behalf, a Volunteer approached Josephine and made her an offer. If she would become a spy for Collins and pass on secret information to him, he would get her children back from Wales. Desperate, she agreed.

Volunteers snatched the children from their grandmother and reunited them with their mother in Cork. In return, Josephine passed on a great deal of secret information. On one occasion she was about to be searched as she left her workplace, but she was tipped off about the proposed search and didn't take any documents with her, thus saving herself from arrest and almost certain imprisonment.

In April 1918, Collins was arrested at his offices on Bachelor's Quay in Dublin. A hostile crowd gathered and threatened the arresting policemen. Michael spoke to the crowd and calmed them, preventing the policemen from being attacked. Before a court in Longford, he was charged with making an illegal speech. Refusing to recognise the court or to accept bail, he was taken to Sligo jail to await trial. This was Michael's second taste of prison.

9

On the Run

Unrest in the country continued. Volunteers openly drilled and large crowds gathered to hear speeches calling for violence as a means to win Ireland's freedom. These gatherings led to clashes with the police. The country was like a barrel of gunpowder waiting for the spark that would set off an explosion.

The British government had helped to create this atmosphere by executing the 1916 leaders. Now, making things worse, they formed a committee to look into drafting a new Home Rule Bill. But this was only a minor error of judgement when compared to the decision to draft a bill introducing conscription into Ireland. Any able-bodied Irish man of a certain age could now be compelled to join the British army and go and fight in Europe.

On the Run

The Irish Parliamentary Party withdrew from the London parliament in protest. Never again would its members sit in Westminster. By the end of the year they would be left with just a handful of elected representatives. This would leave the way open for Sinn Féin and pave the way for Irish independence and a parliament in Dublin, the very thing the Irish Parliamentary Party had been seeking for so long.

At a protest meeting in Dublin, there was united opposition against conscription, and the Irish Parliamentary Party and Sinn Féin, who were bitter opponents, joined together in protest. An anti-conscription pledge was drawn up, and signed by tens of thousands of people.

Matters were drawing to a head and men like Michael Collins, with his great organisational ability, were needed. However, he was still in Sligo jail. He was ordered to accept bail, and travelled back to his office at Bachelor's Walk to begin a new phase in his life. When he failed to appear in court, a warrant was issued for his arrest, and from then on he was on the run.

The British government reacted to the conscription situation by banning Volunteers from drilling. They also banned dances, Irish classes and sporting events. They drew up a plan to arrest all the prominent members of Sinn Féin, and they circulated rumours that Sinn Féin was plotting with the Germans, Britain's sworn enemy. This so-called 'German Plot' was just another ploy to justify their actions.

It was now that Collins' G-men spies proved their worth. Broy and Kavanagh tipped him off that he and the leaders of Sinn Féin were to be arrested. At a meeting, Michael warned all the leaders of their imminent arrest. He suggested that they did not return to their homes that night. De Valera objected. He, like some of the other leaders, was unsure whether the information provided by Michael's spies was reliable. Even if it was, he felt that arrests would give them good publicity. That night, de Valera and most of the leaders were arrested.

Michael, along with Harry Boland, knew the information was genuine and didn't go home that night. Instead, he cycled about the city and witnessed many of the arrests. He cycled to the house of Seán McGarry to warn him, but McGarry had already been arrested. Since the soldiers would not return to McGarry's house that night, Michael slept there.

Now Collins and Boland, two senior members of Sinn Féin, the Volunteers and the IRB, were left virtually in charge of the three organisations. They took advantage of this opportunity, and made sure that their supporters had prominent positions, and that the Sinn Féin candidates in any future election would also support their side.

With the ending of the First World War, in November 1918, there was no further need for conscription. Now only Home Rule remained as an issue to be dealt with. In December 1918, a general election was held. Collins and Boland worked ceaselessly on behalf of their candidates, and Sinn Féin won a resounding victory, taking 73 seats out of 105. The Irish Parliamentary Party, which before the election held 80 seats, took just six. Michael Collins was elected in south Cork.

The people had spoken. They had voted for an Irish Republic that included 32 counties. But in the north, the loyalists and Orangemen were still determined to fight rather than be ruled from Dublin. They had a powerful armed force to back them, much more powerful and better armed than the Volunteers in the south. Matters in Ireland had reached another crisis point.

It is unlikely that Michael Collins really believed that the British would agree to an independent Irish Republic at this time. He was a pragmatic man and must have known that such a possibility would bring about a war with Ulster which would plunge the country into an abyss. What he could best hope for was some form of independence from Britain, certainly something better than just Home Rule. Once Ireland gained that independence, then he could continue to work to bring about a 32-county Irish Republic. However, others in the Volunteers, Sinn Féin and the IRB still held the dream of an Irish Republic. It was a dream that they could not let go.

Collins was now a wanted man. But instead of hiding away, he moved freely about Dublin on his bicycle. He didn't think like a wanted man nor behave like one and this was to be the key to his remaining free. Instead of looking like a frightened fugitive, he resembled a respectable businessman. He dressed in a suit and tie and many times he escaped arrest because of his appearance. The police assumed that a wanted man would be shabbily dressed, unshaven and behaving in a nervous manner. As Michael did not fit their assumption, he was naturally ignored.

He couldn't afford to go into hiding. He simply had too much to do. He was still organising his intelligence network of spies and trying to obtain arms. He was also meeting the leaders of the flying columns scattered about the countryside. The newly-elected Sinn Féin MPs refused to take their seats in London, and instead met in the Mansion House in Dublin on 21 January 1919. Here they formed the first Dáil Éireann. Éamon de Valera was elected President, and Michael Collins became Minister for Home Affairs. Of course, many of the new TDs (Teachtaí Dála) were still in prison.

On the same date, Dan Breen and Seán Tracey, along with other Volunteers, ambushed a group of policemen guarding a wagon of gelignite at Soloheadbeg quarry in Tipperary. Two policemen were killed. This action began what was to be known as the War of Independence.

Collins was laying down plans for the expected war, and setting up what was to become known as 'The Squad', a small group of Volunteers who would execute spies and informers. He had offices about the city and travelled to and from them openly on his bicycle. He worked from dawn until late at night, often seven days a week. He found time for other activities too – he always made time to visit friends who were ill or to help out the families of men who were in prison.

If he were caught, he would most likely be beaten and tortured and then shot. Yet he never hid away, and would often stop at roadblocks or checkpoints to joke with the police or soldiers who were looking for him. He would even dare to complain to them about that fellow, Collins, who was causing everyone so much trouble, and express the hope that they would soon catch him! This was certainly not the behaviour of a man on the run.

Michael also had great consideration for the men who were in prison, making sure that they had cigarettes and messages smuggled into them. He began to plan on getting some of them out. One of those he helped to escape was Robert Barton; a file was smuggled into Barton in Mountjoy Jail and with it he cut the bars on the window of his cell, and climbed out. Once he was outside, he climbed over the wall using a rope ladder thrown to him by Volunteers waiting on the other side.

This success prompted Michael to try again. This time he intended getting two men, Piaras Béaslaí and Patrick Fleming, out of Mountjoy Jail. Again a rope ladder was used, but not only did the two men escape – eighteen other prisoners escaped too! Meanwhile an anxious Michael was waiting for news of the escape. 'Are the two men out?' Michael asked when a man arrived with the news.

'They're all out,' the man replied to Michael's disbelief.

Warders in the jail were prevented from intervening by other prisoners. They held the warders at bay with what appeared to be guns hidden in their pockets. After the prisoners had escaped the guns turned out to be spoons. This caused great amusement both for Michael and the newspapers of the day, which carried the story.

The man Collins most wanted to free was Éamon de Valera, who was being held in Lincoln Jail in England. De Valera would be more valuable as a free man, but it would also be a huge publicity coup for the Volunteers if they could free him.

First of all, de Valera needed a key to open the locks on the doors and get out of the jail into the grounds. A drawing of the lock and key was obtained, and a key was made, but it didn't work. Then de Valera, while serving mass, melted some candle wax. He secretly borrowed the chaplain's master key and made an impression of the key in the wax which was smuggled out and sent to Dublin. This new key, smuggled back into the prison in a cake, did work, and now the escape plan could be put into action.

Collins and Boland travelled to England to take part in the escape. They had a second key with them, with which they intended opening a door in the outside wall. On the night itself they cut through the wire fence around the jail and made their way to the door. Collins put his key in the lock and tried to turn it. To his disbelief, the key broke in the lock. By now de Valera, Seán McGarry and a man called Seán Milroy had reached the door, using their key to open all the locked doors within the jail. However, they couldn't get out if they couldn't open the final door in the wall.

But luck was with them. From the inside, de Valera shoved his own key into the lock. It dislodged the broken key, which fell out, and the door could be unlocked. In a scene which might have come from a comedy film, Boland draped a fur coat over de Valera's shoulders. Then taking his arm, the two walked away from the prison. In the dark they looked like a man and woman and succeeded in making their way to a waiting car and a drive to freedom.

Collins' delight was short-lived. Instead of returning to Dublin, de Valera announced that he was going to America. He felt that there he could gain a great deal of sympathy and money for Ireland's cause. Many in Sinn Féin and the IRB were dismayed, feeling that de Valera's rightful place was in Ireland. He was, after all, their leader. Cathal Brugha was sent to persuade de Valera to return to Dublin briefly before he left for America, to boost morale, and de Valera agreed. By this time an embarrassed British government had decided to release most of the remaining prisoners. They even pretended that they had allowed de Valera to escape.

Collins planned a huge reception for de Valera on his return. This angered the British, and also caused disagreement within Sinn Féin and the IRB, because he had organised it without discussing it with anyone else. Many moderate members were angry, and felt that he was doing whatever he liked without consulting them. The reception was cancelled, but it was a hollow victory for the moderates. They were being pushed further aside by men who believed that only violence was the answer to Ireland's situation.

In April, the Dáil met in the Mansion House in Dublin. Éamon de Valera was elected President, in effect the President of Ireland. Cathal Brugha became Minister for Defence and Michael Collins Minister for Finance. Money would be needed to run the departments and so it was decided to raise a national loan. The job of raising the loan became the responsibility of the finance minister, along with all his other jobs. Collins virtually ran the loan single-handed, despite being the most wanted man in Ireland. It was an enormous undertaking on top of all his other work, and eventually would take its toll on his health.

Now, as he had during his time in Frongoch, he used wrestling as a means of letting off steam. He often wrecked the bedrooms of the safe houses in which he slept, wrestling the men who were staying there with him. He obeyed no rules during those wrestling matches and, if in danger of losing, would resort, as he had so often before, to 'having a bit of ear'. Most of those who knew him accepted this as his way of getting rid of the fear and tension that were his permanent companions. But others, meeting him for the first time, were often shocked. This was hardly the behaviour of a Minister for Finance in the proclaimed government of Ireland. But Michael Collins was no ordinary man. He was an extraordinary man who did extraordinary things during an extraordinary time in Ireland's troubled history. He was a controversial figure too and has remained so since his death.

One role has dogged his reputation, however, and that was as the man who set up and ran 'The Squad'. At any time it numbered no more than about a dozen men, most of them quite young. One of them, Vinny Byrne, was only eighteen. These were to become the most feared men in Dublin. Without them, the War of Independence would probably have had a very different outcome.

They were Collins' men, handpicked by him. They were loyal to him and would never refuse to carry out his orders. They were to be his most ruthless asset in the coming fight with the British and, along with the flying columns, would eventually bring the British government to the negotiating table.

10

The Murder Squads

In June 1919 de Valera left for America. His departure was a double blow for Michael Collins, because he also lost his great friend and ally, Harry Boland. De Valera had insisted that Boland would come with him.

Collins and Boland had virtually run Sinn Féin, the IRB and the Volunteers together. They had obtained arms, run spies, organised and carried out jail breaks and had many narrow escapes from capture. Despite both being in love with Kitty Kiernan, they had maintained a friendship and a working relationship. Now when Collins, already overburdened with work, desperately needed his friend and colleague beside him, de Valera took him away.

Controversy surrounds de Valera's decision to go to America. He felt that political pressure could be brought to bear on the

British government to give Ireland her freedom, and believed that he could persuade the American government to exert such pressure. Millions of Irish and Irish-Americans lived in the US, and no American president or government could ignore them.

Why de Valera insisted in taking Harry Boland with him will never be answered. Did he want to separate him from Collins? Was he envious of their relationship? De Valera sought power and perhaps he saw the two together as a threat to his chances. Boland may have chosen to go – maybe he was jealous of Collins' relationship with Kitty Kiernan. Or perhaps he foresaw the day when he would have to choose between Collins and de Valera and realised even then that he would side with the latter.

Whatever the reasons, Collins now found himself the lone leader in the guerrilla war which had already started. Although Cathal Brugha was Minister for Defence, his dislike of Michael kept the two men apart. Michael was now fighting his own war and he had picked the men who would stand with him and do his bidding. Brugha decided that the Volunteers should swear an oath of allegiance to the Dáil. This was agreed and from then on they increasingly became known as the Irish Republican Army (IRA).

In April, 1919, on a night when the Dáil was sitting, Collins struck a blow that would assist him greatly in the coming fight. Ned Broy smuggled him into Detective Headquarters in Brunswick Street. It was a daring escapade, even more daring in its execution. Broy led Collins to the records room, where were kept the files containing the details of those the detectives were watching. These included Michael himself, along with most of his colleagues. He laughed when he read his own file, but no doubt it was a nervous laugh. Around him in the building were dozens of G-men who would willingly shoot him on sight.

Collins obtained some priceless information that night, probably the most important he ever obtained. Not only did he get access to the detectives' files, but he learned what they knew about him and his colleagues. He also learned a great deal about how they operated and how they collected their information. He realised that if he wished to defeat the British then he needed to deal with the detectives and the spies, the ears and eyes of the government. If he could stop them from operating, he would have dealt a severe blow to the administration in Dublin Castle.

He began to issue warnings to the detectives to stop their activities or suffer the consequences. Some took heed of the warnings, and spied with much less enthusiasm. Others scoffed; who was Michael Collins, a frightened man on the run, to be threatening them?

A number of prominent Americans were in Ireland to see for themselves what was happening. They attended a meeting of the Dáil in the Mansion House and afterwards the G-men, seeking to arrest Collins, raided the building. He was warned of the raid by Joe O'Reilly and both men escaped over a wall into the premises next door. Here they hid in extremely filthy conditions while the detectives, some led by Detective Daniel Hoey, searched the Mansion House from top to bottom. Unable to find their quarry, they had to admit defeat and leave.

When they had gone, Collins and O'Reilly, covered in dust, emerged from their hiding place. While Michael went off to wash, he sent his faithful colleague to bring him his uniform, and prepared to make an appearance that would help confirm his status as the man the British could neither capture nor defeat. That night a reception was held in the Mansion House for the American delegates. Collins, resplendent in his uniform, made his entrance, causing a sensation. Here was Britain's most wanted man appearing in public, in full uniform, in a building which earlier that day had been raided by the detectives seeking him. It helped create another little bit of the legend of Michael Collins.

As Director of Intelligence in the IRB, Collins gathered a number of men around him to help in collecting and assessing information. Among them were Liam Tobin, Frank Thornton and Tom Cullen. He trusted them implicitly. They were loyal and courageous and ready to take on the roles he had chosen for them. They also knew that they would have to carry out actions that would gain them the tag of 'murderers'.

One other man close to Collins, probably closer than any other individual, was Joe O'Reilly. He played many roles in Collins' life

– friend, confidant, servant, nursemaid and messenger. He was the man Collins would shout at when he was roused to grief by the death of a comrade or to anger by incompetence by one of his staff. Many were shocked by the way Collins treated him. Some even complained to Michael and told him that he should leave his faithful servant alone. But O'Reilly never complained and remained devoted to his leader until the latter's death.

Perhaps O'Reilly understood that Michael needed to vent his anger and frustration and indeed his fears. His life was one of constant vigilance. He rarely slept in the same bed two nights running. He had the constant fear that someone – perhaps even someone close to him – might betray him. And he was still doing the work of four men. He worked all hours every day with little time for recreation and no chance to relax. If he dropped his vigilance for one moment, it could spell disaster.

With his intelligence men and the Squad ready and armed for action, Collins continued to accumulate the sort of information he needed. What he wanted was information on the G-men who had not taken heed of his earlier warnings. His spies spoke to maids and barmen and hotel staff and railway workers – anyone who could help them. Slowly but surely they began to build up their own files, much like those Michael had seen at Brunswick Street. Through his cousin Nancy he continued to gain access to files at Dublin Castle. Others in positions of trust around the country also supplied information. Michael was like a spider at the centre of a web, its threads reaching out to anyone who could help him.

By the summer of 1919 the police had become more brutal in their dealings with anyone they saw as a threat to the government. This led to even greater unrest throughout the country. The people began to boycott the police, who often retaliated against innocent citizens. Some flying columns then hit back against the police and the level of violence slowly but surely worsened.

Collins now acted against the G-men. It was not retaliation, but for a practical reason – to remove a threat to his guerrilla war against the British. Being a detective was a specialist occupation. A detective needed to know his working environment, and to build up trust and a network of informers. If a G-man was eliminated he could not be easily replaced, unlike a soldier or a normal policeman. Eliminating the G-men would cut off the information which was so vital to the British administration.

They were given warnings first. Mostly, these were verbal warnings given to the men as they patrolled the streets. At other times, members of the Squad called at their homes to warn them. One detective, Constable O'Brien, was gagged and tied to railings and told to stop his activities. He and many others did listen to the warnings, but other detectives refused to be cowed. One of the bravest and determined of these was a man known as 'The Dog ' Smith, a particularly brutal man. He had been asked to drop charges against Piaras Béaslaí, but refused. Now the Squad singled him out for the first killing. Issuing the order to shoot Smith was probably the most difficult decision Michael Collins had had to make. Killing Smith was not the same thing as shooting a soldier in battle. It would mean shooting a man to death in cold blood. There would be no opportunity for Smith to surrender, nor would he be given the opportunity to fight back. Instead, Volunteers would approach him and shoot him dead.

The Squad did not yet officially exist, and was not acknowledged until late September 1919. In the beginning it was led by Mick McDonnell and then by Paddy Daly. Other members were Joe Leonard and James Conroy. Later Mick O'Reilly and the young Vinny Byrne, one of the most ruthless of them all, joined as well. For days before the killing, members of the Squad watched Smith's movements. At night they lay in wait for him. As Smith walked home on the night of 30 July 1919, the Squad opened fire on the detective with .38 revolvers. Smith was hit a number of times but still managed to draw his own gun and return fire. He ran for his home, reached it and staggered inside, locking the door behind him. He survived that night, but was so badly wounded that he died later of his injuries.

Collins was affected by the killing on two counts. Firstly, it upset him that a man, no matter how dangerous, had to be killed in cold blood. He was also concerned that Smith had managed to get away. From then on the Squad would carry .45 revolvers, with greater killing power than the .38s. It may seem a callous and cold-blooded decision, yet was perfectly logical in the circumstances. If you intend to kill a man, then you had better do it in the most efficient way you can.

The killing of Smith shook the British administration. They banned Sinn Féin, raided its headquarters and seized documents. They also banned the Dáil. These measures only angered the people of Ireland even more. They had voted for Sinn Féin, and its members were their legally elected representatives.

Collins decided to kill another detective in response. Daniel Hoey had picked out Michael's friend, Seán MacDermott, for imprisonment after the Easter Rising, and he had also led the raid on the Mansion House when Collins and O'Reilly had barely escaped capture. In September 1919, Hoey was shot dead outside the police station in Great Brunswick Street. His killers were armed with .45 revolvers, and Hoey had no chance to fight back or escape. With these two killings, the Squad became officially recognised.

Meanwhile, violence increased in other parts of the country. Dan Breen and Seán Tracey were involved in the killing of a policeman while rescuing another Volunteer, Seán Hogan, at Knocklong Station in County Limerick. Slowly but surely a reign of terror was gaining momentum.

During this hectic time, Collins faithfully visited the family of Éamon de Valera every week, bringing them much-needed money and offering comfort to a wife and children who were missing a husband and father. Despite being constantly hunted by the British authorities and their spies, he managed to plan another daring jailbreak, at Strangeways Prison in Manchester, where Piaras Béaslaí and Austin Stack were prisoners. Using an assumed name, he visited Stack in the prison and planned the escape with him.

On the night of 25 October 1919, while some Volunteers stopped the traffic on the Manchester streets, Stack, Béaslaí and two other prisoners climbed over the wall and reached the ground via a ladder provided by other Volunteers. They were then brought to the Manchester docks and returned to Ireland by boat. Stack was ill and took some time to recover. He had to remain in bed and Collins, again despite his heavy workload, regularly visited him.

The British commission set up to examine the issue of Home Rule made its report. It recommended that the British government should try to resolve the Irish question speedily. But Britain did not want Ireland to leave the empire, which was already under threat. If Ireland left, other countries would also demand to leave.

The other main problem was Ulster. The loyalists were ready and willing to fight for their own parliament in Belfast. Britain could not allow Ireland to become a 32-county republic, but it could not enforce the Home Rule Act either, which had promised an all-Ireland parliament sitting in Dublin. Certain counties in Ulster would have to be excused and given their own parliament, while Ireland as a whole would remain within the British Empire.

11

The Black and Tans

By 1920, violence had spread to all parts of the country. Even small villages in remote areas were not exempt from killings and the burning of homes and places of work. The IRA was still a small force and still poorly armed, but a majority of the people were on their side. With that kind of support they could achieve much more than a heavily armed force without local support.

Despite being small in number, the IRA decided to go on the offensive. Using guerrilla tactics, they struck suddenly and silently at the enemy before slipping back into the general population, which gave them shelter and help. Many of these ordinary people became the eyes and ears of the guerrillas. They passed on vital information, carried messages and smuggled arms, often at great risk. Without them, the war might well have had a different outcome.

The Black and Tans

While Michael Collins had the Squad to carry out killings, the British also had groups of men who were willing to kill in cold blood, known as 'murder gangs'. They were ruthless in their methods, each man aware that at any moment his fate could be sealed with a bullet through the head. Worse still was the possibility of being captured. If that happened, a man would be tortured to obtain whatever information he might have before being shot. It was a fear that all of these men on both sides lived with, yet most stuck to their task with great courage and determination.

The year 1920 began with the IRA in Cork openly attacking British barracks on New Year's Day, led by Tomas MacCurtain and Terence MacSwiney. Other members in the south followed suit and martial law was declared in many areas. This meant that military law took over from the proper legal system, and courts martial were held instead of trials.

On 15 January local elections were held, the first in many years. Sinn Féin did even better in these elections than before, showing that the people were fully in support of what they were trying to achieve. Even in the north, many Sinn Féin members were elected, including Michael Collins. Many local councils which were now controlled by Sinn Féin decided not to give their allegiance to the British administration, but to the Dáil. In Cork, Tomas MacCurtain was elected Lord Mayor with Terence MacSwiney as his deputy. The British administration was slowly losing control.

On 20 January a policeman was shot dead in Thurles, County Tipperary. In response, the British military drove through the town, firing their guns and terrifying the locals. This pattern of shooting and reprisals was to become common during the coming year.

In March, a letter was sent to Tomas MacCurtain threatening his life, written on notepaper stolen from one of Michael Collins' offices. Clearly it was intended to show that there was dissent between the IRA and Sinn Féin. Some days after the letter was delivered, another policeman was shot dead in Cork. That night police surrounded MacCurtain's home and armed men with blackened faces burst in the door. They shot MacCurtain dead in front of his wife.

The authorities tried to blame the IRA for the killing, but the inquest declared that MacCurtain had been murdered by policemen on the orders of the British government. The blame for the killing could ultimately be placed on David Lloyd George, the British Prime Minister. Collins was greatly affected by the killing of MacCurtain. He realised that the British were willing to use any means at their disposal, even the murder of an elected Lord Mayor, to defeat the IRA. It also meant that his life was in even graver danger than before.

The British government was embarrassed by the publicity and the condemnation surrounding the murder of Tomas MacCurtain, but it didn't stop the murders from continuing.

The Black and Tans

And as they realised that they could not defeat the IRA with the forces they now had in the country, they decided that new forces were required.

Two separate groups of law enforcers were now created. In reality they were to obey no law and were in fact to be a law unto themselves. Their names became a byword for murder, violence and oppression. These were the Black and Tans, commonly called the Tans, and the Auxiliary Cadets, better known as the Auxies.

The Black and Tans were recruited from men who were unemployed. Many of them had fought in the First World War. When the war ended, they signed up to go to Ireland and fight the IRA. Their uniforms were a mixture of army khaki and police black. As a result they got the nickname 'Black and Tans', as the colours were similar to those of a pack of hounds of that name. They were sent to fight terror with terror and were given a free hand to bring the country under control.

They soon began to terrorise the local population. They would enter a town or village and open fire on houses and people. They shot animals in the fields and burned homes and buildings. Soon they became both dreaded and hated throughout the country.

But if the Black and Tans were a brutal and violent force, the Auxies were even worse. These were mostly ex-army officers who had also fought in the First World War, hardened men who were not afraid of fighting. As ruthless as the Black and Tans, they were also nevertheless courageous. While the IRA feared and loathed them, they also admired their bravery, seeing in these men a reflection of their own courage. The Auxies wore a blue uniform with a Glengarry cap, a kind of beret with a distinctive cap badge. They were probably the most brutal force ever sent to Ireland and they became the most menacing force in the country.

They were the visible evidence of British policy in Ireland. They were everywhere and their presence on the streets of the cities and towns made everyday life for the citizens extremely difficult and dangerous. Yet despite their strong presence in Dublin, Michael Collins went about his daily routine, cycling around the city on his bicycle. He travelled to his various offices and safe houses, often passing through roadblocks manned by Tans and Auxies who were actually looking for him. He had many narrow escapes. However, the police did not have a good photograph of him and so he was not easy to identify.

While the Auxies and the Black and Tans openly terrorised the country and sought out the rebels and their leaders, an intelligence war was also being fought. This was the war of the spies.

12

Murder by the Throat

One of the British spies sent to Dublin to try and trap Michael Collins was a man known as Jameson. His real name, however, was Burns. He was short and stout and middle-aged. He claimed that he sold musical instruments, and he had an interest in keeping birds. He got to know some Irish people in London by pretending to be a communist who wanted to support Ireland's fight for freedom. He offered to try and get arms for the IRA, and claimed that he could create disunity among the British forces.

Collins actually liked Jameson, but the others who met him distrusted him. A number of incidents – one of which was that the British learned that Michael was growing a moustache – eventually aroused suspicion of Jameson, because he was one of only a handful who knew of the moustache and could have passed on such information.

But Jameson was much more dangerous than anyone imagined. He set traps for Collins and almost succeeded in capturing him. On one occasion British agents almost captured Collins when he took Jameson to meet Mrs Batt O'Connor, wanting to get her opinion of him. A detective was watching the house. When he saw Jameson come out with another man, he thought the man was Collins, but Collins was still in the house. The detectives, who were about to raid the house, didn't do so. If they had, they would have found Collins with Mrs O'Connor, who told him she did not trust Jameson.

Michael learned of this narrow escape from his own spy, James McNamara, who had been with the party of detectives intending to raid the house. McNamara had also heard Redmond, the man in charge, claim that one of the spies had actually met Collins, although he had only been in Dublin a short time. The spy referred to by Redmond had to be Jameson.

Jameson would have to be killed, as would Redmond, the new head of the detectives. He had been sent to Dublin from Belfast to reorganise the detective division, but no one knew what he looked like, so Collins sent Frank Thornton to Belfast to get a photograph of him. Led by Paddy Daly, the Squad shot Redmond outside the Standard Hotel in Harcourt Street on 24 January 1920. Horrified and angered by this blatant murder, Dublin Castle offered a reward of £10,000 for information leading to the capture of the killers and the men who gave them their orders.

Jameson had now to be taken care of. He had obtained guns for the IRA, and handed them over to Thornton at 56 Bachelor's Walk. Thornton pretended to hide the guns in the basement while Liam Tobin led Jameson away, but instead he took them to another building on Bachelor's Walk. Thornton, Tobin and Cullen then watched 56 Bachelor's Walk to see what would happen.

That afternoon the building was raided, but of course no guns were found. That night the soldiers returned and dug up the basement. This meant that they must have been very sure the guns were hidden there. Now Collins knew that Jameson had to be a spy, and had tipped off the authorities that the guns were on the premises. Jameson was picked up by members of the Squad on 2 March and told he was being taken to meet Collins. Instead, he was taken to Ballymun where he was shot dead. Jameson showed great courage, insisting that he was proud to die for the king.

But there were other spies willing to take his place. One of the most important of these was Harry Quinlisk, once a British soldier. He had been helped by Collins, who had given him money and clothing and lodgings in a house in Mountjoy Square. Later, this house was raided, perhaps a sign that Quinlisk had given the address to the detectives. Collins was willing to believe that it was just a coincidence.

Whether or not Quinlisk was a spy from the beginning, he certainly became one, and wrote to Dublin Castle offering to sell them information on Collins and others, but Ned Broy informed Collins of this. A trap was now set. Quinlisk was told that Collins was in Cork, staying at Wren's Hotel, and the authorities sent a secret message to the police in Cork ordering them to surround the hotel and arrest him. Quinlisk travelled to Cork to collect the reward on offer for the arrest of Collins, who of course was safe in Dublin and now knew that Quinlisk was a spy. The Cork IRA caught up with Quinlisk in the city, took him out into the country and shot him.

Another spy who met a similar fate was Brian Mulloy, a British soldier who worked for a British intelligence officer named Colonel Hill Dalton. Mulloy knew Thornton and Cullen and they often drank together in Kidd's Back, a bar used by members of the British Secret Service. In fact many of them often chatted with Cullen, Thornton and Tobin without knowing who they were. Mulloy offered to get the three men into Dublin Castle to see the secret files held there, but they were already suspicious of Mulloy and declined his offer. They were aware that once inside they would not come out alive.

Instead they suggested that Mulloy help them kill Colonel Hill Dalton. Immediately Hill Dalton moved his address, clear evidence that he was warned of the plan to kill him. Only Mulloy could have told him. Collins gave the order for his death, and he was shot in the street near the Wicklow Hotel. Also shot at this time was the porter at the hotel, William Doran, who was an informer. His widow, seeking help to raise her children, asked Sinn Féin for a pension and Collins, who had ordered the shooting of her husband, arranged this.

Despite many close escapes from capture, and the fact that there were spies everywhere and an enormous price on his head, Michael still took time off to go to the theatre, to the races or to Croke Park for football and hurling matches. Often he would mix in hotel bars with the very men who were hunting him.

The war in the country continued. Flying columns ambushed convoys of Black and Tans or Auxies and then slipped away back to the countryside, where the locals hid them. The IRA also shot informers and spies and those who assisted the British forces. There was disagreement between Brugha and Collins, because Brugha believed that the IRA should openly fight the British, but his tactics would have been disastrous. The IRA were few in number, badly armed, and there were only a handful of professional soldiers among them. The only advantages they had were the element of surprise and local knowledge. Their war had to be a guerrilla war if it was to have any hope of success.

Instructions were given to the British forces to shoot on sight anyone who even seemed suspicious. One man who gave such instructions was a Colonel Smyth, in charge of the Tralee district. The IRA learned of his decree and decided to deal with him in the same way. Smyth was found by the IRA in Cork and shot dead.

A terror had been unleashed and no one could say where it would end. Whenever a British soldier or policeman was killed, the Black and Tans and the Auxies took revenge. They burned houses and whole streets in villages and towns. They also began to follow a new policy, intended to damage or destroy Ireland's economy. Creameries were burned to the ground, as well as factories, mills and shops. At times the Tans and Auxies went berserk, often drunk on stolen alcohol. No one was safe, and many civilians were shot dead at random.

Despite outrage in Ireland, and indeed in Britain itself and abroad, the British government continued to pursue its policy, leading to, for example, the burning of Balbriggan in County Dublin, Sligo town and other towns in Munster. Anyone captured by the British forces was usually tortured, often horrifically, and then shot dead. This helped to create and enforce the atmosphere of terror.

Those involved in these atrocities were often later shot on the instructions of Michael Collins. He needed to show the Black and Tans, the Auxies and the police that whatever they did, they did at their peril. It was also intended to show the British government that the IRA could not be cowed or beaten into submission. What is less understandable is the attitude he took towards those who gave information under torture. Anyone who did so was liable to be shot. Perhaps it shows how ruthless he had to be in a war that was to become known for its ruthlessness.

He still needed his own informers and those who could supply him with vital information. Whenever he found such a man or woman he made use of them. Gerry Maher, a clerk in County Kildare, had access to the secret codes used by the police. Through the breaking of the codes, Collins learned the names of some of those who had taken part in the murder of Tomas MacCurtain. One of them, Detective Inspector Swanzy, had gone to the north of Ireland, probably thinking he would be safe there. He was sadly mistaken. In August 1920, Michael Collins sent men to the north, and Swanzy was shot dead.

The IRA also suffered casualties. Men like Tom Hales and Pat Harte were captured in Cork and mercilessly tortured. Many of those captured were murdered. Seán Tracey, who with Dan Breen had fired the first shots in the war at Soloheadbeg in January 1919, was shot dead in a gunfight in Talbot Street in Dublin. Kevin Barry, an eighteen-year-old medical student who had been involved in an ambush of British soldiers, in which three were killed, was captured, tortured and hanged in Mountjoy prison. Collins had planned to try and rescue him, but had to call off the attempt due to the large crowd that had gathered outside the prison to pray.

Not all of them died through a bullet, or under torture, or at the end of a hangman's noose. The Lord Mayor of Cork, Terence MacSwiney, went on hunger strike in Brixton prison in London to protest against his imprisonment, but the British government refused to release him or other prisoners they were also holding. After 74 days on hunger strike, MacSwiney died. Two others on hunger strike also died. These deaths made news around the world.

MacSwiney's funeral in London brought huge publicity and sympathy for Sinn Féin and for Ireland's cause. MacSwiney was buried on 31 October 1920, and his funeral brought the country to a standstill. There was nothing the British authorities could do about it.

Lloyd George still gave the impression that Britain was winning the war. They had, he said in November 1920, 'murder by the throat' in Ireland. But he was very mistaken.

13

Bloody Sunday

Michael Collins knew it would only be a matter of time before he was captured. Thornton, Cullen and Tobin had already been arrested and released, but he, or they, might not be so lucky next time. The British had brought in agents from abroad. Many of these had worked in Cairo, in Egypt, and were nicknamed the 'Cairo Gang'. They were not only spies, but had also been involved in the shooting of some of Collins' men. They would have to be dealt with.

Most of them lived in houses around the city without any protection, apart from whatever gun they carried. Servants in the houses and others supplied information, and files were prepared on each agent. A list was drawn up and a date chosen for action, Sunday 21 November 1920, soon to be called 'Bloody Sunday'. A football match was being played in Croke Park between

Dublin and Tipperary. There would be a large crowd in the city for the game, so the Squad would be able to blend into the crowd while they went about their murderous task.

Early that Sunday morning, in groups of two or three, the killers entered the houses where the agents lived. Keys had been obtained beforehand, or else a servant let them in. The agents were then singled out. Many were still in bed at this early hour. They were shot, sometimes in front of their wives who pleaded for mercy. But no mercy was shown. Each man was gunned down in cold blood. By the end of the morning, about a dozen agents had been shot dead.

When news of the killings reached Collins, he suggested that the football match in Croke Park be called off, but it was too late for that. The match went ahead. While it was in progress, British forces surrounded Croke Park. With armoured vehicles, they entered the ground. Once inside, the Black and Tans and the Auxies opened fire on the crowd and the players with machine guns and rifles. Fourteen people were killed and a great many injured. One of those shot dead was a Tipperary player, Michael Hogan. To honour his name, one of the stands in Croke Park is named the Hogan Stand.

The authorities claimed that the soldiers had only opened fire after the IRA had fired on them. But as no Black and Tan or Auxie was killed, or even injured, it seems obvious that the soldiers were not fired on. They had indeed opened fire in revenge for the earlier killings. Later that day they killed another innocent man, along with two of Michael Collins' most stalwart men. The innocent man was Conor Clune, not a member of either the IRA or Sinn Féin. He had been arrested on the Saturday night during a raid on Vaughan's Hotel. The two Volunteers arrested were Dick McKee and Peadar Clancy.

They were held in Beggar's Bush Barracks, completely at the mercy of the Tans and the Auxies. Already drunk, these were driven wild with their desire for revenge that Sunday, and all three prisoners were mercilessly beaten and tortured. On Sunday night they were shot dead. As their bodies were being loaded onto a lorry, an officer battered their faces with a torch, so demented was he with rage.

When Collins learned of their deaths he was utterly grief-stricken. Though the city was in a state of absolute terror, he insisted on going to see the dead men in the mortuary chapel. Here he helped to dress the two IRA men in their uniforms. Then he ordered that the coffins be closed so that relatives would not see the bruised and battered faces of their loved ones. Collins also insisted on attending the funerals, and helped to carry the coffins. It was a foolhardy act. He could have been arrested at any moment. This gesture showed not only his courage, but also his loyalty to his men and his grief at their terrible deaths.

The British claimed that the secret agents were shot because they were trying to bring criminals to justice. They did not admit the truth – that the secret agents were in fact killers, just like those that had killed them. The incident at Croke Park was also blamed on the IRA – the British were merely trying to capture dangerous criminals when they were fired on from the crowd, and had only fired back in self-defence. It was never made clear how none of the soldiers were killed or injured. Clancy, McKee and Clune were apparently shot trying to escape.

The reality was that the British were badly shaken. They had been very close to capturing Michael Collins, whom they saw as the leader of the war. If they had captured him, they would not only have struck a great propaganda blow against the IRA and Sinn Féin, but also removed the brains behind the war. Now they had lost in one morning many of their spies and killers, their most potent weapons.

That Sunday's terror nevertheless struck a blow against Michael Collins as well. What had happened to the three captives struck fear into many of the IRA, as well as those who acted as messengers and gatherers of information. Many went into hiding while others refused to co-operate any more. Collins still went cycling about the city as usual, passing through roadblocks and checkpoints. It was a dark time for him. He had not only to contend with the atmosphere of fear and danger in Dublin, but also the loss of his friends. The innocent deaths in Croke Park were also hard to bear. The murders of the British agents preyed on his mind. He would have been aware that they too had killed men in cold blood, but it was not easy to dismiss so many deaths on one day. In his mind, as in the minds of many others, it certainly had been a Bloody Sunday and he had been the man most responsible for it.

How many more would have to die before the British gave in? Michael simply did not know. Nor did he know if he could force the British to concede before he was captured or before the IRA should fail. This war could not go on forever. In the end the superior forces of the British Empire would prevail, as they had done so often before.

But for now he would fight on. For now, the IRA would fight on.

14

A Vicious War

In November 1920 one of the most daring ambushes of the War of Independence was carried out at Kilmichael, near Macroom, in County Cork. A flying column, commanded by Tom Barry, ambushed a convoy of Auxies and Black and Tans at a remote place. Seventeen of the enemy were killed. One of the planners of the ambush had been Michael's brother, Johnny, also known as Seán. Later in the following year the British forces would take revenge on the Collins family.

But they would take revenge on Cork city long before that. In December 1920, following another ambush, Black and Tans and Auxies began a spree of looting, killing and burning in Cork. City Hall was burnt, and premises on Saint Patrick's Street were also set on fire. Again the British government denied that their forces were to blame, though it was quite clear they were responsible. The Black and Tans and the Auxies were doing exactly what they had been sent to Ireland to do. They were terrorising the local population so that they would be too fearful to support the IRA. Without local support, the IRA could not function.

The burning of houses and creameries continued. Bridges were blown up, causing great inconvenience to the local population. People were arrested and harassed. Cattle were driven off or killed. There were continual reprisals on both sides; it was terror piled on terror with neither side willing to yield.

As the year of terror drew to a close, de Valera returned from America. His time there had been successful in raising funds for the National Loan, but he only allowed half of what he had collected to be returned to Dublin. It seemed that even in the matter of money, he didn't trust Collins. There was never any evidence that Michael had ever misused monies entrusted to him. In fact, he had done Trojan work with the National Loan.

When a danger arose that the British authorities would locate and confiscate the National Loan funds, Michael acted in his usual ruthless manner. A man named Bell had been brought out of retirement by the British authorities to try and trace the funds kept in the banks. Aware that Bell would eventually find most of the money, Collins ordered that he be shot. Bell was caught on a tram one morning on his way to work and was shot by the Squad. But despite this, and the ample evidence that Michael was dealing honestly with the monies from the loan, de Valera still did not appear to trust his comrade.

De Valera had been less successful in getting American support for Ireland's demands for freedom. His cold, aloof personality worked against him, and he caused some disagreement among American groups who supported the cause. Now back in Dublin, he was not at all happy to be told that 'The Big Fellow' had managed matters quite well while he had been away. He tried to persuade Collins to go to America. This was simply a ridiculous idea, as without Michael Collins, the war would falter. Collins was bitterly upset at this and so were many of those he worked with. Only Brugha and Stack supported de Valera, as both would have been glad to see the back of Collins.

While de Valera had been in America, Michael had been acting as president in his place. Now de Valera appointed Stack as his president designate. This was clearly a snub to Michael, as Stack was an ineffectual man, according to many of those who knew and worked with him.

Boland and Michael renewed their friendship. By now Kitty Kiernan had fully transferred her affections to Collins, and Boland seemed to accept this situation, but he must have been upset. Whether this had any bearing on his subsequent split with Michael can never be answered. Certainly while in America he came under the influence of de Valera and his ideals, so perhaps it's not surprising that he later sided with his leader.

Collins was now leading a life more fraught with danger than before. The number of times he barely escaped capture increased.

A Vicious War

He was simply following Joseph Plunkett's advice that if you behave as if you're not being hunted, then those who hunt you will not recognise you. On Christmas Eve, while Michael and a number of others, including Tobin and Cullen, were having dinner at the Gresham hotel, the Auxies raided the premises. Michael was searched and his notebook was found on him, along with a bottle of whiskey, which he claimed was a present for his landlady. He was questioned about the notebook but managed to give some likely explanations for some of the entries. He asked permission to go to the toilet and was accompanied there by one of the Auxies. When he didn't return, Tobin went to investigate. He found the Auxie checking Michael's appearance against a photograph. It was not a good photograph, and eventually Michael was released.

Back in the dining room, the Auxies had opened the bottle of whiskey. Michael promptly ordered a second one and in an atmosphere of Christmas cheer, they all drank to each other. It was a very close encounter for Michael and showed how easily he could be captured.

Others who helped him were not so lucky. One of these was Eileen McGrane. Her flat was raided on New Year's Eve and important papers were discovered. She served time in prison in England. Ned Broy had typed up some of the discovered papers and came under suspicion, but Collins managed to warn off the officer who was investigating Broy. He also persuaded another man to flee, therefore throwing suspicion on him. As a result, Broy escaped almost certain torture and death.

In the new year of 1921 the narrow escapes continued. The Mespil Road home of Eileen Hoey, a supporter, was raided. A revolver was found and she was taken to Dublin Castle. Later she was driven back and the Auxies and Tans set a trap for Michael. He was due to call at the house and Eileen realised that she had to warn him. She persuaded her elderly mother to pretend she had had a heart attack, then pleaded with the soldiers to allow her to get a doctor. Speaking in Irish to him, she managed to give him a warning for Collins. The doctor pretended to attend to her mother, then got a message to Collins. Michael was stopped just in time from visiting the house. However, the raiders obtained a great many valuable documents and papers. Eileen Hoey was imprisoned, where she suffered greatly. Only after the truce in July 1921 was she eventually released.

Through the first half of 1921, the war continued, as bitter and vicious as before. Tom Barry led another successful flying column operation at Crossbarry in County Cork, inflicting heavy casualties. One of the most successful flying columns was that commanded by Seán MacEoin, a blacksmith from Ballinalee, County Longford. He defeated the enemy on many occasions, often with just a handful of men. Cathal Brugha felt that MacEoin was wasted in the countryside and called him to Dublin, but on his return journey he was arrested in Mullingar.

During the arrest he was shot and then badly beaten, so severely that he was given up for dead. He survived, however, and Collins, who greatly admired him, planned an escape. A first attempt failed when MacEoin became ill and was moved from his cell to the hospital wing.

A second attempt involved the hijacking of a British armoured car by the IRA. At Mountjoy Prison, dressed in the uniforms of British soldiers, they bluffed their way into the prison. Emmet Dalton and Joe Leonard went to the Governor's office, claiming to have orders to collect MacEoin and take him to Dublin Castle. Meanwhile, out in the prison yard, a sentry became suspicious and opened fire on the armoured car. The men in the armoured car returned fire, and the sentry was shot. Dalton and Leonard, with their cover blown, tied up the Governor and his staff and made their escape back out to the yard. By now a machine gun had opened fire and under a rain of bullets the two men ran for the safety of the armoured car. They managed to scramble aboard and all got safely away.

Collins did not manage to help MacEoin escape from prison, but so strong was his admiration for the man that he made his release a condition of the truce he would agree with the British later that year.

One of the most brutal acts of murder occurred at Clonmult, County Cork. Here, a force of Black and Tans and Auxies surrounded a group of IRA men in a thatched cottage. A fight raged for some hours and when the cottage caught fire, the IRA men agreed to surrender. They were promised that they would be treated fairly if they surrendered, but the Tans and Auxies went berserk. Nine of the IRA men were beaten to death and the remaining six were arrested, court-martialled and sentenced to death. While women prayed outside the walls of Cork prison, the men were executed by firing squad, one by one. In retaliation for this, the IRA shot dead six British soldiers in Cork.

In April 1921 Michael Collins was dealt a personal blow in this vicious and bitter war when his old home at Woodfield was burned to the ground. His brother Johnny lived there with his children, his wife having died. Now he and his children found themselves homeless. Neighbours and relatives took in the eight children, but even in this situation, some people were frightened of helping the family in case of retaliation by the Tans and the Auxies. Johnny Collins was arrested the day after his home was burned and sent to Spike Island prison. Here, due to medical neglect, he lost the use of his right hand.

This personal tragedy for Michael Collins did not deter him from his path. It made him even more determined to continue the fight, despite the opposition coming from de Valera and Brugha. Both men still thought that the IRA should take on the British forces in open battle.

On 25 May 1921, de Valera decided to apply this tactic. On his orders, a group of Dublin IRA men attacked and burned the

A Vicious War

Custom House. Although the building was destroyed, it was a disaster for the IRA. Many of those who took part were captured, reducing the small number of men Collins had at his disposal. It was a military disaster, as Collins had predicted. Yet it caused great damage to the administration in Dublin Castle due to the loss of files and documents, especially those relating to tax affairs. It also focused worldwide publicity on Ireland and on the war being fought there.

This attack was to be the last major offensive of the war. But it did not stop the violence, and around the country the burning of houses and businesses by the Tans and Auxies continued. The IRA retaliated by burning the homes of loyalists. This brought protests from those who saw themselves as loyal to Britain, and who were now suffering as a result. The British government ordered a halt to the burnings which helped to ease this particular problem.

In May 1921, local elections were held. Sinn Féin won a resounding victory, a sure sign that the people were behind them despite the ongoing war and the suffering it caused the ordinary people of Ireland. In Ulster James Craig won an equally resounding victory. The country was utterly divided, and a border was already being drawn.

In 1921 the Tans and Auxies adopted a new method of preventing their lorries from being attacked. They took Sinn Féin members as hostages, and tied them to posts in the lorries.

Now the IRA could not attack the lorries without the risk of killing their supporters. To counteract this, Brugha suggested kidnapping members of the British parliament and holding them hostage. He had always advocated taking the war to Britain, but Collins had opposed this. Now, though, he did consider it, but then the taking of hostages stopped as suddenly as it began.

By the middle of 1921, both sides were beginning to tire of the seemingly endless war of murder and retaliation. The British were coming to realise that this was a war they could not win. What they didn't know was that the IRA and Michael Collins were also tiring. Many IRA men had been killed in the conflict. Many more had been wounded or were in prison. They were fighting with what arms they possessed or could take from the enemy, often with limited amounts of ammunition. They could not go on fighting at this extreme for much longer.

Just as Collins was planning a major attack on secret agents, Tans and Auxies in Dublin, he received a message directly from Lloyd George, the Prime Minister of Great Britain. He was willing and ready to end the conflict. He wanted peace.

Collins and his small group of IRA men, poorly armed and facing death every day of their lives, had brought the might of the British Empire to its knees. They had effectively won a war as vicious and as brutal as any ever fought in Ireland. Now only one question remained. Could they win the peace and achieve

what so many before them had tried to achieve and failed –
freedom for Ireland?

15

The Truce

Before there could be peace, there had to be a truce. The British demanded that the IRA give up their arms, but the IRA refused on the grounds that this would appear like surrender. There was also the question of immunity for Michael Collins. He was described by the British as a murderer and still had a price on his head. A third problem was the release of prisoners like Seán MacEoin.

The authorities in Dublin Castle were opposed to any form of truce. They still believed that they could defeat the IRA and capture Collins. They felt that a truce would favour the IRA, who could use the opportunity to rearm and regroup. They suggested an all-out offensive to destroy the IRA, but the government ignored them, and the three problems were eventually sorted out.

The Truce

The IRA would not give up its arms. Michael Collins was granted immunity. MacEoin and other prisoners were released.

On 11 July 1921 the truce came into force. On this sunny summer's day the British army, Black and Tans and Auxies withdrew to their barracks. Their withdrawal left the streets and the countryside free at last. Collins and his small band of freedom fighters had won. Now they would have to win another battle – that of obtaining their aims from the British government.

This would be no easy task. They had little experience of negotiations while the British had vast experience in this area. There was a lot of opposition to any talks, especially from Tory MPs in the British parliament. There was also the problem that Lloyd George had stated that he was willing to negotiate anything that fell short of an Irish Republic. What might be on offer was Dominion status within the British Empire, like that of Canada. There was opposition to the truce on the Irish side too. Many thought they should fight on. They believed they had the British on the run, and could drive them into a corner where they might be more willing to accede to any demands made. Collins himself was nervous of the truce. Once it came into force, the IRA men could return to their homes and families. Many of those who had lived lives on the run would now be recognised and noted by the authorities. If the truce failed and war began again, they would no longer be anonymous. Neither would he. He also had grave doubts that he could trust the British. They had behaved treacherously in the past and might do so again. Lloyd George was first and foremost a politician, not a soldier, and Collins felt that politicians could not be trusted.

In July, de Valera travelled to London with a delegation to meet Lloyd George. Among the delegates were Arthur Griffith and Austin Stack, but not Michael Collins. De Valera claimed that he did not want the British to get a good photograph of Michael, which might well have been his intention in leaving him at home. Or maybe like a good poker player, he realised that Michael could still be an ace to be held in reserve.

This apparent rebuff distressed and upset Collins. He, more than anyone, had brought about this opportunity. While de Valera was in America, safe from arrest and torture and death, Michael had lived in constant danger day and night. Now he was being sidelined at this vital and historic moment in Ireland's history.

But the general population was jubilant that at last there was peace. The people had suffered greatly over the past years and now they were at the dawn of a new era for Ireland. They could sense it, and they were optimistic. They could not imagine that the country could ever return to war, but that was still a real possibility if the peace talks broke down.

In a meeting with Lloyd George, it was made clear to de Valera that he could not have an Irish Republic. Here already was one problem that seemed destined to cause serious difficulties in any negotiations. But an even more serious difficulty was the question of Ulster. James Craig was satisfied with Ulster's own parliament in Belfast. He stated in public that he did not care what agreement de Valera and Lloyd George came to over the 26 counties, as long as Ulster had its parliament in Belfast.

Lloyd George drew up a draft treaty offering Ireland Dominion status for 26 counties. The new state would recognise the state of Ulster, which would not be forced into a 32-county Ireland without the consent of the majority living there. De Valera was made well aware that any settlement would fall well short of an Irish Republic.

In August, de Valera rejected Lloyd George's offer and the Dáil endorsed this. He stated in public that the Dáil did not have the force to defeat Ulster, nor would he wish to use force if he had it at his disposal. Any county which did not wish to be in the new republic could opt out by voting for such a course of action. He was coming to realise that Ulster could not be forced to become part of a republic.

Lloyd George now invited an Irish delegation to talks in London. De Valera insisted that Michael Collins should go to the talks while he stayed at home. Collins did not want to go and at first refused. He was a soldier. He felt he could not negotiate with statesmen like Lloyd George and his team. De Valera was the statesman. He was the leader of the Irish government. He was the one who should go and lead the talks.

Collins felt that he would be of more value at home. If he wasn't with the delegation, then they could use him as a threat against the British. They could demand more concessions during the talks by pretending that it was Michael Collins who was making the demands. They could use the threat that if he did not get his way he might restart the guerrilla war which had brought about the talks in the first place.

Michael didn't realise what this claim of his importance implied for de Valera, who saw himself as the only Irish leader. Collins was claiming that he was the one responsible for bringing the British to the negotiating table. This angered de Valera and made him more determined than ever to have his way. He had the casting vote and voted that Michael Collins should go. But even then he had to get Michael's friends and comrades to persuade him to go.

Why de Valera made this decision to send Michael Collins to the Treaty talks, and remain at home himself, will never be known. He claimed that the presence of the soldier Collins would make the British anxious to agree to a treaty, because they did not wish to return to war. But it really was de Valera's place to have gone to the talks. As the head of Irish government, and recognised as such around the world, his place was at the negotiating table. He had already met Lloyd George. He knew what he was up against and would have been in a better position to negotiate than anyone else.

The Truce

Many believe that de Valera sent Collins because he knew that the British would never agree to what was being demanded. They would not allow an Irish Republic, or let Ireland leave the Empire, and they would not agree to force Ulster to accept rule from Dublin. Collins would fail to get what was being demanded and could be blamed for this, leaving de Valera free from blame because he wasn't there.

If this was so, it was a very cynical move indeed. It was also a big mistake, because it weakened the Irish delegation's negotiating ability. Tragically, in light of later events, it also left de Valera free to oppose the Treaty when it was eventually signed, ultimately leading to the Civil War.

Eventually Collins agreed to go. The negotiators who went with him were Arthur Griffith, Robert Barton, Éamonn Duggan and George Gavan Duffy. They were given complete freedom to negotiate, and were ordered to report back to the Dáil on how the negotiations were progressing.

Griffith was reluctant to go, and informed de Valera before he went that the negotiating team could not obtain a republic nor get the British to agree on Ireland leaving the Empire. It is certain that de Valera was already well aware of this, and he suggested that they should negotiate for 'External Association' with the British Empire. This was his own proposal, and meant that Ireland would associate with the other Dominions, but outside the Empire, without owing allegiance to the monarchy.

Griffith was ill at this time. Though he was the recognised chairman of the negotiating team, Collins carried the bulk of the work. He was the one who returned regularly to Dublin (a long journey by train and mailboat) to inform the Dáil of how the talks were proceeding, but he was also feeling the effects of a life of overwork and of constant fear and tension.

He had taken his most trusted agents and men to London with him, including Liam Tobin, Tom Cullen, Ned Broy and Emmet Dalton. They stayed at 15 Cadogan Gardens whilst most of the delegation stayed at 10 Hans Place.

Negotiations opened on 11 October 1921. De Valera described his team of negotiators as representatives of the elected government of the Republic of Ireland. He already knew that the British would never agree to a republic, but he still seemed to regard the republic as already in existence. He was refusing to accept the real situation. Perhaps he was already planning for the future; when Collins and his team returned without a republic, de Valera could blame them for the failure.

De Valera himself later said that one day the Irish people would hold Michael Collins in the very highest regard, and that this would be at the expense of his own reputation. In this assessment he was almost certainly correct.

16

Signing a Death Warrant

The Irish and British delegations met at Downing Street on 11 October 1921. Lloyd George led the British delegation, which included Lord Birkenhead and Winston Churchill. Later reports of the negotiations make clear that they regarded Michael Collins as their toughest adversary.

The British soon became aware that there was disunity among the Irish delegates. De Valera later stated that he had deliberately chosen the members so that there would be disunity among them. If this was so, then it was an extraordinary thing to have done at one of the most important moments in Ireland's history. The British were also aware of the feelings of the Irish people, who were tired of war after suffering greatly from the hostilities over the past number of years. Since the truce, life had been slowly returning to something like normality. The people welcomed this and would not be willing to support further war.

The British must also have known that the IRA were not in a position to continue the war with the same ability and determination. With all these advantages, the British were able to drive a hard bargain. Collins told his old friend, Joe O'Reilly, that no matter what he achieved during the negotiations, it would still be regarded as insufficient. He implied that de Valera would make this judgement, and that Brugha and Stack would support their leader.

This situation certainly did not bode well for the coming negotiations, the most important ever to take place on behalf of the Irish people. Collins knew that what he saw as being achievable would not be acceptable to de Valera and his supporters. He saw any treaty as a stepping stone to his ultimate goal – a 32-county Irish Republic that would not owe any allegiance to a British king. He knew that it would take time. It was his tragedy, and that of Ireland, that he did not have the support of all his comrades, and died before he could achieve his dream.

The talks were not without other problems. Spies were operating on all sides. De Valera had Erskine Childers, a secretary with the delegation, sending secret reports back to him. As part of the negotiations, many of those taking part met privately for discussions, often at social functions. Collins met Winston Churchill on a number of occasions at the home of the artist, Sir John Lavery and his wife Hazel. It has been claimed that Lady Lavery and some of those friends who met at her home were spies reporting back to the British delegation. Though there is no proof of this, it is likely that some were in fact reporting back to the British government, or at the very least offering their views on those they met and spoke with.

So it was that the vital talks to decide the future of Ireland were carried out in an atmosphere of distrust on both sides. Meanwhile, those who had remained behind in Dublin did not trust those whom they had sent to negotiate. It did not bode well for the negotiators or the negotiations.

There were other problems. In Ireland the truce, while generally holding, was sometimes broken by both sides. The IRA was attempting to obtain arms and was involved in incidents of gunrunning. Brugha was involved in one of these incidents and caused Collins and his delegation serious problems. There was a failed attempt to obtain arms from Windsor Barracks in England. The British blamed Collins for this, but he and Griffith were able to defuse the situation and the talks continued. Collins again tried to persuade de Valera to join the talks, but he refused.

Both sides slowly came to agreement on what might be regarded as minor issues. But one major problem was the question of an Irish Republic, which the British were vehemently opposed to. Another was the wording of an oath of allegiance to the king, and Ireland's position within the empire. And looming above those two problems like a dark cloud of fear was the question of what should be done about Ulster.

James Craig was willing and able to fight for what he had –
an Ulster with its own parliament in Belfast. In this he had the
support of the majority of the Protestants in Ulster. Just as
important, he had support in Britain, especially from the Tory or
Conservative Party, the opposition to Lloyd George's Liberal
Party. Many influential people in Britain also supported Craig.
They believed that no part of the British Empire should be
forced out of that empire against its will.

All sides were aware of what the failure of the talks would
mean – war would recommence. Collins knew that if war began
again it was likely that the IRA would be defeated. He also knew
that the British would be even more ruthless, if possible. Martial
law would be introduced throughout the country, making the
waging of a guerrilla war all the more difficult. The people would
no longer give their full support. Ireland would lose much
influence and goodwill both in America and throughout the
world if it was thought that they were the ones responsible for the
failure of the talks.

There were many compromises during the talks. Griffith
suggested that instead of a republic, Ireland should be regarded as
a Free State. The British agreed. There was a compromise on the
wording of the oath of allegiance to the British king, and it was
agreed that a boundary commission would be established to set
the boundaries of the Ulster state.

Eventually a draft agreement was drawn up, and it was

discussed in the Dáil. There were bitter arguments on its merits. Brugha was against it. Ulster remained a major problem, even for Collins himself. There, violence was increasing as loyalists murdered Catholics and drove them from their homes.

The Irish delegation returned to London. Lloyd George was willing to give way on the wording of the oath if the Irish would accept Dominion status. There was deadlock. Lloyd George now stated that he was going to announce that the conference was over. That meant war. The Irish delegation was faced with a stark choice. Either accept the agreement and sign, or return to war.

In Dublin the Black and Tans and Auxies were back on the streets. In London, the British spies were more active than ever. Shadowy figures followed the Irish delegates and hung about Hans Place and Cadogan Gardens. In turn, they were shadowed by Collins' own men. If the agreement was rejected, it was likely that the British would try to arrest Collins and the other IRA men with him. As a precaution against this, arrangements were made to have a plane standing by to fly them out of Britain before the spies could arrest them.

The Irish delegation returned to Hans Place in the evening of 5 December to discuss what they should do. Collins, Griffith and Duggan were for signing. Barton and Duffy were opposed. The argument raged for hours and eventually all five decided to sign. Around 2 a.m. on the morning of 6 December 1921, the Irish delegation returned to Downing Street. Here, Michael Collins and the four other members of the team signed the Treaty. Lord Birkenhead said that he was probably signing away his political future, but Collins prophesied, 'I have signed my own death warrant'.

Michael Collins had achieved part of his dream. Twenty-six counties of Ireland were about to gain independence for the first time in over 700 years. But for some of those who had fought in the war, this was not enough. Ireland was about to enter another bloody phase in her long and troubled history, but this time it would be Irishmen killing Irishmen in a bloody and brutal civil war.

17

A Divided Country

The Irish delegates returned to Ireland. While many regarded them as successful heroes, to others they were traitors. Nasty rumours began to circulate concerning Michael Collins. It was claimed that he was about to marry Princess Mary, a member of the British Royal family, which upset him and his fiancee, Kitty Kiernan. Other rumours claimed that he was in love with Lady Lavery. There was talk of drinking and wild parties at Cadogan Gardens. No doubt there was some drinking, and some parties did take place. Michael and the other delegates were involved in difficult negotiations, and needed some recreation, but the stories were wildly exaggerated.

One of the most ridiculous rumours was that Michael was a British spy. This hurt him greatly. For years he had been at the forefront of the war. He had been a hunted man, rarely staying in the same house two nights running. He had helped many of those who now turned against him. Many of them had once praised his kindness, friendship, loyalty and capabilities. Now they were willing to believe the rumours, and indeed to make up some of their own.

There was deep division in Ireland over the Treaty. The press was in favour, as were the majority of the people who wanted peace and not war. But the opposition was there, and it would grow. De Valera first saw the details of the Treaty in a newspaper. He was furious, and when the Treaty document was eventually handed to him, refused to read it. This was not because he rejected it, but because he had not been consulted before it was signed.

At first the delegates didn't know who would support them. Collins knew that Brugha and Stack would certainly oppose the Treaty, and that de Valera would not like it either. He hoped de Valera would come to accept it, and he also expected Harry Boland would be on his side. But he was wrong.

After the negotiating team returned to Dublin, heated Dáil debates on the Treaty took place, up until Christmas, and again at the beginning of January. There was great bitterness on both sides, and those opposed to the Treaty denounced Michael Collins at every opportunity. He was both angered and devastated by these attacks, but he was fearful too. If the Treaty was rejected, it could lead to civil war.

A Divided Country

Arthur Griffith, Joe O'Reilly, Frank Thornton, Robert Barton, Tom Cullen and other loyal colleagues continued to support the Treaty. Éamon de Valera, Harry Boland, Cathal Brugha, Austin Stack and Rory O'Connor opposed it. It hurt Collins greatly to find himself now shunned by those he thought his friends. At times he was reduced to tears, at others to towering rage. If another war broke out many of those whom he still regarded as his friends and comrades would die. He also knew only too well that his own death was very likely.

Debate on the Treaty raged not only in the Dáil, but throughout the whole country. There was hardly a person who didn't have an opinion on it. Everywhere people were divided, even within families.

The vote was taken in the Dáil on Saturday 7 January 1922. There were 64 votes in favour and 57 against. Griffith was with Michael Collins. Michael's old friend and comrade and wrestling partner, Harry Boland, was with de Valera. Collins pleaded with de Valera and his supporters not to be hasty. They needed to stick together for the moment at least – the country needed them. But de Valera now offered his resignation, and with his supporters left the Dáil. Boland went with him. Michael Collins was bereft.

On Monday 9 January there was another debate in the Dáil, but there was to be no reconciliation between the opposing parties. When a vote was taken to reinstate de Valera as President, it was defeated by 60 votes to 58. De Valera and his supporters again left the Dáil, after bitter and heated exchanges. Arthur Griffith was elected President in his place. He appointed Michael Collins as Minister for Finance, the post he had already held in the illegal Dáil. Under the Treaty, a Provisional Government was set up. Michael became its Chairman while Griffith remained as President of the Dáil.

As Chairman of the Provisional Government and Minister for Finance, Michael was kept busy. He had to oversee the drawing up of a new constitution for Ireland. Added to this, the British wished to hand over Dublin Castle and other sections of the administration, and it was his job to oversee this too. There was growing unrest in Ulster, where Catholics were still being murdered by loyalists. And all the time, opposition to the Treaty was increasing.

Many in the IRA were were becoming more hostile towards it. Their hostility is perfectly understandable. These were the men who had fought the guerrilla war. They had lived on the run for years, hiding in ditches and outhouses, cold and hungry, and always in danger. They had seen their colleagues tortured and killed, and their homes burned to the ground. They had been fighting for an Irish Republic made up of 32 counties. Now they were being asked to accept a Free State of 26 counties. They would also have to swear allegiance to the King of England. For many of them with families steeped in the Republican tradition, it was simply impossible for them to accept the Treaty. They would rather fight and die than accept.

On January 16 1922, Dublin Castle, the most potent symbol of British rule in Ireland, was handed over to Michael Collins. He was seven minutes late for the handover and managed to joke with the British that, as Ireland had waited over 700 years for this moment, seven minutes hardly mattered.

Elsewhere in the country, other barracks were also handed over. Many of these were taken by anti-Treaty IRA members. These were to become known as Republicans, while soldiers loyal to the Provisional Government became the Free State army.

Collins wanted to prevent a split in Sinn Féin over the Treaty, as well as a split within the IRA. But the country was at boiling point. In Limerick there were tensions between pro- and anti-Treaty supporters. Violence was only avoided when both groups agreed to leave the city. But the anti-Treaty forces were preparing for conflict, and there were episodes of violence in other parts of the country. Anti-Treaty forces seized many barracks. They also attacked pro-Treaty forces to obtain arms. A ship carrying arms was boarded off the Cork coast and arms captured, supposedly by Tom Barry and his men, who had fought at Kilmichael and Crossbarry. Tactics used in the guerrilla war against the Tans and the Auxies were now used against the Free State soldiers. If civil war were to break out, it would be bloody and brutal.

On 23 March, Ulster reached a new crisis point when one of the worst atrocities of all took place. Armed men, part of the security forces, broke into the home of the MacMahon family. John MacMahon, his four sons and a lodger were lined up and shot. Four of the victims died instantly. John MacMahon and one of his sons survived. The murders caused outrage both in Ireland and Britain. No one was in any doubt that the killers were members of the security forces. Collins' reaction to the incident was to arm the IRA men who were active in Ulster. This was a clear breach of the Treaty, but he felt he had no other choice.

As yet there was no outright declaration of civil war, or a really serious incident that could lead to war. But on 14 April, all that changed. Rory O'Connor, now the leader of the Dublin anti-Treaty IRA, seized the Four Courts building in the centre of Dublin. Here he set up his headquarters. De Valera in his speeches supported the rebels, which undoubtedly gave them confidence.

O'Connor's action was an open challenge to the Provisional Government, but Collins did nothing yet. He was still trying to avoid bloodshed, and almost certainly hoped that common sense would prevail, and civil war would be avoided. The fact that he did not act against the rebels undoubtedly gave them the impression that he had grown soft, and that they could eventually defeat him and the Treaty.

A Divided Country

De Valera broke off talks at the end of April. He wanted to delay the election which was due to be held. To prevent further conflict, a group of Free State army officers suggested that a coalition government should be formed. They also arranged talks with both sides in an attempt to prevent outright war, but the talks were unsuccessful. In Kilkenny, Republicans seized some buildings in the city. These were retaken by the Free State soldiers, as was Kilkenny Castle. In other parts of the country, clashes between rival factions continued.

In May, Collins signed a pact with de Valera. They agreed that no election would be held at present and that a coalition government should be formed. This was totally against the provisions of the Treaty. Griffith was horrified, but agreed to the pact for the sake of peace. In Britain it was condemned. Many of Collins' supporters were opposed to it. Griffith was both angry and saddened by the events. He felt that action should be taken against those opposed to the Treaty. He urged Collins to attack the Four Courts and drive out the rebels.

But Collins would do anything to prevent war. This is understandable when one considers the sort of war he had just fought. He had ordered cold-blooded killings, but he had seen those killed as the enemy. In a civil war he would be fighting and killing his own countrymen, many of them his former friends and comrades.

18

Civil War

By now Arthur Griffith was a broken man. He had given his life for Ireland. Now he did not know at what moment he might be shot as a traitor. Collins too was suffering. He was physically ill, and the strain was taking its toll on him. He was no longer the man he had been, but he continued to make attempts to ease the tensions. At a ceremony attended by both pro-Treaty and anti-Treaty supporters, Michael had arrived late. The two groups stood apart until he picked up a cork, and threw it at the anti-Treaty group. Within minutes both groups were throwing corks at each other, and then a wrestling match ensued between them. But soon they would be engaged in a very different confrontation.

Unrest and violence in Ulster continued. Loyalists were murdering Catholics on a daily basis, burning Catholic homes and forcing Catholic families to flee. It seemed as if the Protestant majority wanted to clear all Catholics out of the province. Collins was still helping the IRA in Ulster who were fighting on behalf of the Catholic population. He supplied them with arms, thus reducing the fighting power of his own Free State army. This was a betrayal of both the Treaty and the British government, but he felt that he could not stand by and allow the Catholics in the north to be murdered.

In June, Griffith went to London with the new constitution which had been drawn up. The British government rejected it, creating yet more problems. Growing opposition to Ireland in Britain was being led by men like Henry Wilson, a former soldier who supported Craig in Ulster. Collins was being attacked from all sides.

An election date was set for the 'Pact Election' on 16 June. The people of Ireland would decide if they agreed with the Treaty or not. Collins travelled the country speaking in favour of the Treaty. He was continually in great danger from his enemies, and often violence was only prevented through the intervention of local people. On a number of occasions, those who opposed him tried to stop him from speaking. Michael's bodyguards protected him on these occasions, though there were times when he met his enemies face to face, and forced them to back down.

De Valera was also travelling about the country. He claimed that if the present situation continued, then there would have to be civil war. If only de Valera and Collins could have worked together, much more serious conflict could have been avoided.

In the election the Republicans held only 36 seats, losing 22 seats. Griffith and Collins won 58 seats, losing eight. Most of the seats lost were taken by parties like the Labour Party and the Farmers' Party, which both supported the Treaty. Despite this endorsement of the Treaty, events were occurring which were to lead to serious confrontation between the two sides.

On 22 June two IRA men, Reggie Dunn and Joseph O'Sullivan, shot dead Henry Wilson outside his London home. No one knew who had ordered the killing. Collins came under suspicion because he had met Sam Maguire shortly before that, and it was Maguire who had recruited Dunn and O'Sullivan. O'Sullivan had a wooden leg and could not run away afterwards. Dunn refused to leave him, and both men were captured. Collins did everything in his power to save the lives of the two men, even asking the British to release them, but the British refused.

Naturally, the British government was appalled at the killing of Wilson. They suspected that the IRA men who now held the Four Courts, and who were opposed to the Treaty, had sent the killers. This could be correct, as Rory O'Connor had also met Maguire prior to the killing. Britain now made it clear that the Provisional Government would have to deal with the rebels in the Four Courts, but Collins still hesitated.

On 26 June, Free State soldiers arrested some of the Four

Courts rebels when they attempted to seize trucks and fuel. In retaliation, the rebels kidnapped General O'Connell of the Free State army. The following day they also seized other buildings in Dublin. Rory O'Connor also now proposed that the IRA should attack British soldiers still in Ireland. He hoped this would draw the pro-Treaty soldiers into a fight, thereby undermining the Treaty, and probably leading to its failure. O'Connor's statement was virtually an open declaration of war and could not be ignored. Michael Collins and his government would have to take action. Churchill made it clear that if the Provisional Government would not, or could not, deal with the rebels, then the British army would deal with them.

Collins had to take action. He was furious, because it would look as if he was acting under orders from Britain. It was an intolerable situation, and he must have wished, not for the first time, that he'd gone to America in January 1916, and forgotten about Ireland and her problems. He now demanded the evacuation of the Four Courts. It was refused, and at 4 a.m. on 28 June the Free State army began its attack on the building. Civil war had begun.

It bore an uncanny resemblance to the British attack on the GPO in 1916. Shells screamed though the air, there was the rattle of machine-gun and rifle fire. But now it was Irishmen fighting Irishmen, friends against friends, and family against family. For days the bombardment continued. People gathered on the quays to watch. The end was inevitable, and it came on 30 June with the surrender of the rebels. Before they surrendered they blew up the Public Records Office, destroying valuable manuscripts and records going back hundreds of years.

O'Connor and another leader, Liam Mellowes, were arrested. Cathal Brugha, who had joined the rebels, escaped. He and his men were surrounded in the Hammam Hotel, in Sackville Street. When the end was inevitable, Brugha ordered his men to surrender. Then he charged out of the building brandishing his revolver, determined to fight to the end. It was how he had fought in 1916 when, in a similar stand-off, he had been seriously wounded. He was called on to surrender but refused. A volley of shots rang out and Brugha fell, mortally wounded. When Collins heard the news, he wept. He had fought with Brugha in 1916, and had worked with him over the past years. He had been Michael's strongest critic and opponent, but he knew that Brugha had had Ireland's best interests at heart, and in the end had died as he had lived, a brave soldier.

Another who would soon die was one of Michael's greatest friends, Harry Boland. He was caught in a hotel in Skerries on 31 July by Free State troops and was shot in the stomach. He died in hospital three days later and again, Collins wept at his death.

A week after the Four Courts was taken, Collins became Commander-in-Chief of the Free State army. Throughout the country the Free State troops went on the offensive. Cork city was captured from the Republican forces, as were many other towns and strongholds, including Cashel, Clonmel, Limerick, Sligo, Waterford and Tralee.

In many cases there was little fighting, because the Republican forces withdrew to fight a guerrilla war in the countryside, as they had done against the Tans and Auxies. Limerick saw some of the fiercest fighting around the city, as well as in Kilmallock and Newcastlewest. In August, Michael Collins travelled to Limerick and then onto Tralee to view his troops.

While there he had more bad news. On 12 August, Arthur Griffith died when a blood vessel burst in his brain. He was just 51 years of age, but looked like an old man. He had given his life to Ireland and to a dream of seeing her free. He had never sought power for his own sake, and indeed had given up the chance of power on many occasions. Now he had lived to see his own countrymen kill each other. It was the final terrible blow.

Michael Collins returned to Dublin and marched at the head of Griffith's funeral. He looked magnificent, but inside he was being torn asunder by what was happening. On the very day of Griffith's funeral, 16 August 1922, Reggie Dunn and Joseph O'Sullivan were hanged in Wandsworth prison in London. Collins had tried desperately to save their lives, but had failed. Now that failure preyed heavily on his mind.

On that day he had less than a week to live, and it would seem likely that he had a premonition of his own death. He said to a colleague: 'Do you think I shall live through this? Not likely!' He asked his old friend O'Reilly, one of the few who had stood by him through it all, if he would like a new boss. O'Reilly, faithful to the end, naturally said no.

Michael planned to travel to Cork, hoping to meet some of those he had known. He probably hoped they could come to some agreement on making peace. De Valera was also in Cork at this time, and there have been suggestions that the two men had agreed to meet to discuss possible peace moves. There is no evidence of this, but it is possible. It has also been suggested that de Valera had something to do with Collins' death, but there is no direct evidence of this either. De Valera had long since opposed guerrilla warfare and would surely not have agreed with an ambush. He believed that soldiers should fight in open battle. It is unlikely that he would have sanctioned an ambush of Michael Collins, though he might have been willing to shoot him in an open battle if he got him in his rifle sights.

Many of those around Michael urged him not to go, but he laughed at their worries. No Corkman, he declared, would kill him in his own county. They might disagree with him, but they would never kill him. Early on the morning of 20 August 1922, Michael Collins left Dublin for the last time.

19

Michael Collins is Dead

Joe O'Reilly, looking from his bedroom window, saw Collins leave on that August morning. O'Reilly thought that he looked dejected. In fact he wasn't well – he had a cold, and was suffering with stomach problems. Joe, ever faithful, ran downstairs to say goodbye, but when he reached the street the convoy had already left. It was the last time he would see his old friend alive.

The military convoy travelled to Limerick, inspecting troops on the way. From Limerick they went on to Mallow and then to Cork city. At the Imperial Hotel, where he was to stay for the night, Michael found two sentries asleep on duty, and banged their heads together. He wanted to inspect his army in Cork and discuss the situation there, and also go home to see his people. But he had another reason for his visit, apart from the possibility of negotiating some truce or peace agreement. The Republicans in Cork had been collecting taxes on their own behalf and Michael wanted to recover the money, which was badly needed by the Provisional Government. He stayed overnight in the Imperial Hotel. The next day he met his sister Mary and his nephew. Later he travelled to Macroom to inspect troops there. He returned to Cork city later that day, and seemed to be in better spirits.

On the morning of 22 August, Collins' convoy left Cork city to travel to west Cork, where he had been born and reared. Lieutenant Smith, a scout on a motorcycle, led the convoy. Behind him came a Crossley tender, a lorry containing soldiers with rifles and machine guns. With them were Joe Dolan and Seán O'Connell, both of whom had been members of the Squad. There may have been a second Crossley tender with the convoy, carrying more soldiers along with some IRA men from County Mayo who wished to join the newly formed Civic Guard. Michael Collins travelled with General Emmet Dalton in an open touring car. Bringing up the rear was a Rolls Royce armoured car nicknamed 'Slievenamon'.

The convoy travelled to Macroom, passing through the village of Coachford. In Macroom, Michael met Florrie O'Donoghue, who had been captured by Free State soldiers and was now imprisoned there. O'Donoghue was a local Republican leader and Michael met him to discuss a way to bring about a truce. From Macroom the convoy went onto Bandon.

Trees had been felled to block roads and some bridges had been blown up, so progress was slow. The touring car developed engine problems, and they had to detour more than once, at one point having to ask for directions. The man they asked directions from was Denny Long, who was acting as a lookout for a group of Republicans meeting in the area. Denny wasn't long in reporting the presence of Michael Collins to them. One of the Republicans, local commander Tom Hales, decided that it was too good an opportunity to miss, and he arranged to ambush the convoy on its return journey. The spot chosen for the ambush was Béal na mBláth.

Collins and his party went onto Bandon. From there they travelled further west to Clonakilty. Here the whole town turned out to meet them and honour their returning hero. He had gone away as an innocent fifteen-year-old boy to work as a lowly post office clerk in London. Now he was back as Commander-in-Chief of the Free State army, one of the most important and powerful men in Ireland.

The convoy travelled to Sam's Cross, and then on to Lisavaird, where Denis Lyons had once helped sow the seeds of nationalism in a small boy. It is likely that Michael also met the blacksmith, James Santry, who had also helped to form the man Michael had become. At the recent wedding of Seán MacEoin, Michael had taken MacEoin's pipe as a present for Santry, and this was probably now delivered.

Michael also visited Woodfield to see the ruins of his old home, burned by the Tans. He met his brother Johnny and other relatives. Then they retired to the bar at the Four Alls, where Michael stood rounds for everyone. This was Michael's home place. These were his people. They had known his parents and had known Michael as a young boy. He had come home to meet them.

The convoy travelled onto Rosscarbery and to Skibbereen. Here a photograph was taken of Michael leaving the Eldon Hotel, and it still hangs there along with other memorabilia of his visit and his life. After leaving the hotel, the convoy set out for Cork city, again going via Rosscarbery, where they stopped in Callinan's pub.

There was a row here between Michael's escort and some locals, but it was soon smoothed over. Michael was warned of rumours that an ambush had been planned for Béal na mBláth, but he dismissed them, again claiming that his own people would never kill him in his own county. Back in his home place he seemed a changed man. He was more relaxed, joking with his old friends. He was not the Michael of the Dublin years, when he had been hunted night and day. Now he had relaxed his vigilance.

The convoy returned that evening to Bandon where Michael met Seán Hales, a local commander. Leaving Bandon, they headed back again through Béal na mBláth. The more direct route would have been to take the main road to Cork through Innishannon, but the convoy intended to return the way it had come. This may have been because Michael is supposed to have arranged a meeting with a Canon Tracey of Crookstown. He was hoping that the Canon might act as an intermediary with Republicans in the area, with a view to arranging some kind of truce.

A week before Collins' visit to the area, the Canon's housekeeper had boasted that an important man was coming to meet him. Locals were given to understand that this was Collins. An ambush was planned for a place called Farran, and is alleged to have been in place by 22 August. Locals had known that Collins was going to pass through, so some Republicans could have known of his presence well in advance.

The fact that an ambush was arranged in Béal na mBláth early on that day surely meant that the ambushers knew that Michael would return that way. They must have had good reason to believe that he was not going to take the direct route to Cork, the quickest, surest and safest way back. The convoy had been on the road since dawn, yet they took this longer, more difficult and dangerous route, and moreover a route on which they had been lost earlier that day.

Was this route taken simply to meet Canon Tracey? Or had Michael arranged to meet someone else? Éamon de Valera was in Béal na mBláth earlier that day. Some claim that he watched the convoy pass through. Had he and Collins arranged to meet to talk peace? Or had de Valera arranged to have his chief enemy killed? There is some evidence that, in fact, de Valera tried to stop the ambush and failed. Angry at his failure, he had then left the area, aware that there was nothing else he could do. Perhaps he sent the warnings Collins received about the ambush. No one will ever know.

In Bandon, Collins had said goodbye to his old comrade, Seán Hales. At Béal na mBláth, Seán's brother Tom was lying in wait to kill him. Here, with those two men, the whole tragedy of the civil war was being played out. During the War of Independence, Seán and Tom Hales and Michael Collins had been united in a common dream. Now they were bitter enemies who would willingly kill each other.

Hales and his ambush party, about 30 men, had been in place for most of the day. They had blocked the road with a dray, a large cart. They had also laid mines in the roadway. Men with rifles were placed on the high ground on either side of the narrow road. However, as evening fell, the ambush party decided that Michael Collins was not returning their way. They assumed that he had either taken the direct route to Cork or had stopped off somewhere for the night. Most of the ambush party withdrew. Tom Hales stayed behind along with some others, including Dan Holland, Sonny O'Neill, John O'Callaghan, Tom Kelliher and Jim Hurley.

At this point, Hales decided to take the fuses out of the mines that had been laid in the road. Farmers would be using the road the next day, and he did not want anyone to be hurt or killed. It was while Hales was defusing the mines that the convoy arrived, surprising everyone. Smith, the motorcycle scout, skidded into a ditch as he came upon the dray. Just past it there was an abandoned cart with a donkey grazing the roadside grass. Its owner had abandoned the cart earlier that day when he couldn't get past the barricade. He had argued with the ambush party, but they had refused to move the dray out of his way.

The men on the high ground had seen the convoy, and fired shots to warn Hales. He managed to jump over the fence and find cover. He knew that his group was no match for the convoy, because they had machine guns while his men were armed only with rifles, and were totally outnumbered. But the first shots had been fired.

What happened next would depend on the convoy. The correct procedure would be to drive on as fast as possible. When ambushed, you didn't stop unless it was absolutely necessary. Emmet Dalton gave the order to Corry, the driver of the touring car, to drive on, but Collins countermanded the order. As the convoy had approached Béal na mBláth, he had picked up his rifle, as if expecting trouble.

Now he tapped Corry on the shoulder and ordered him to stop. 'Jump out and we'll fight them,' he declared. These were the words of a man who had lost the sense of danger which had kept him alive for so long.

Were they also the words of a man who was slightly drunk? It is known that drink makes for bravado, and lessens the sense of danger. The members of the convoy had been in many pubs that day. They certainly had been drinking. But as Michael was ill with stomach ulcers, it seems unlikely that he had been drinking. Testimony from those who were with him suggest he was not drunk, but others with him may have been.

The convoy now returned fire. Jock MacPeak in the armoured car opened fire with his Vickers machine gun. His gunner's mate was not with him that day, so one of the other officers fed the belts of ammunition into the gun. But as MacPeak moved up and down the road, firing at the attackers, the gun jammed.

Collins had taken cover behind his car. From here he fired on the attackers. Outnumbered and outgunned, they started to retreat. Michael saw them running away, and urged his own men to redouble their efforts. Leaving the cover of the car, he ran back along the road. From here he would have a better view of the retreating men. He was now out in the open, standing up and firing his rifle, a perfect target for any man who was even a fair shot with a rifle. The men of the ambush party were some of the best guerrilla fighters in County Cork and would hardly miss such a target at such close range.

As the attackers retreated, the shooting eased. Then there came a terrible cry. Michael Collins had been shot. He fell in the roadway, a huge gaping wound in his skull, just behind his right ear. Dalton and O'Connell rushed to his aid. O'Connell said an act of contrition, and thought that Michael squeezed his hand. Then they dragged him back to the cover of the armoured car. Here Smith, the scout, though he himself had been shot in the neck, bandaged the wound.

Collins did not speak. He was dying, if not already dead. He was carried to the open touring car. Here Emmet Dalton held Michael in his arms as they left Béal na mBláth, after first seeking help in the local pub where earlier that morning they had stopped to ask for directions from Denny Long. The fight had lasted no more than 40 minutes at most.

It was a terrible journey back to Cork. The convoy took a number of wrong turnings and, when forced to cross some fields, had to abandon the armoured car, which got stuck in the mud. Then the touring car broke down, and it too had to be abandoned. Michael's corpse, for he was dead by now, had to be carried to the Crossley tender, and in this way they all returned to Cork city.

Collins' body was taken to the hospital at Shanakiel, on the outskirts of Cork city. This was a British military hospital, still staffed by British personnel. Why was Michael taken to such a hospital, and not to one of the hospitals in Cork city? There are many conspiracy theories surrounding the death of Michael Collins, who shot him and why, but these questions will never be answered.

Michael Collins

The only certainty is that on the evening of 22 August 1922, Michael Collins was shot dead in Béal na mBláth. His death was a tragedy for Ireland and its people.

20

Ireland's Greatest Hero

Michael Collins was dead. The stark news travelled to Dublin and to London. In Dublin, the first person to learn of Michael's death was his friend, Gearóid O'Sullivan. He now told others, including Joe O'Reilly and Tom Cullen, with the words, 'The Big Fella is dead'. At first there was disbelief, then grief and tears. Even Michael's most bitter foes were shocked and saddened by the news. In Kilmainham Jail the Republican prisoners, Michael's most hostile enemies, knelt and said the rosary for the repose of his soul.

His sister Hannie was at work in London when she was told of her brother's death. She was devastated at hearing the news, remembering the young boy who had come to London seventeen years before. She set out to travel to Ireland for his funeral. When Kitty Kiernan heard the news she became hysterical with grief. In the space of a few weeks the two men she had loved, Michael Collins and Harry Boland, had died violently. Now Kitty was bereft and alone.

On board a steamship, the *Classic*, Michael's body was brought from Cork to Dublin. The ship's tricolour flew at half mast as a mark of respect. As the ship docked in Dublin, a large crowd had gathered. Many wept openly. As the body was carried from the ship, the wailing from the crowd grew louder.

Michael's body was taken to St Vincent's Hospital, where he was dressed in a new Commander-in-Chief's uniform. He was laid out in the chapel where a few weeks before his great friend, Harry Boland, had also been laid out. His body was later taken to City Hall, where some of his old colleagues formed a guard of honour. Here, thousands came to pay their last respects.

On Sunday evening, Michael's coffin was taken to the Pro-Cathedral. The next day he was given a state funeral. His coffin was draped with the Irish flag, and carried on a gun carriage, drawn by six black horses. Officers in the Free State army and members of the government followed the cortege, as did many dignitaries. Hundreds of thousands of people lined the streets in an outpouring of respect and terrible grief. He was buried at Glasnevin Cemetery, and General Richard Mulcahy gave the funeral oration.

Over the coming months, violence increased as the civil war grew more vicious and cruel with each passing day. The list of those who died grew longer and longer. All of them at one time had been Michael Collins' friends and comrades. Now Seán Hales, Rory O'Connor, Erskine Childers and Liam Lynch all died, either in fighting or before a firing squad. After the death of Liam Lynch, who had been the leader of Republican resistance in Munster, Frank Aiken became their leader, but by now the Republicans had lost heart. They realised they could not win, and Aiken ordered them to give up the fight. The civil war ended, but its effects would live on for generations.

Had Michael Collins lived, would Ireland have been a different country? It is certain that he would have done his best to end the civil war. With his undoubted influence, charisma and strength of spirit and personality, it seems likely that he would have brought an end to the hostilities after a short time. He was a man who did not hold grudges. He would have welcomed reconciliation with those who had fought against him.

Instead, following his death, Free State government troops and Republican guerrillas continued to fight a bitter and brutal civil war. Both sides were involved in terrible acts of violence, and of revenge against each other. Free State soldiers murdered Republican prisoners, as British forces had done in the previous years. Now the Irish government used the same methods against the rebels that the British had used, methods which members of the government had roundly condemned at the time. No matter how ruthless Collins might have been, he would hardly have advocated such methods of revenge and retaliation.

Michael Collins

Although the British had promised that the Boundary Commission would draw a new border in Ulster, this did not happen. The commission reported in 1924, and left the existing border in place. This meant that the one-third of the population that was Catholic and nationalist remained under the Belfast parliament led by James Craig. The Catholics were forced to live as second-class citizens in what they regarded as their own country. Their plight was ignored by both the British and Irish governments, as well as the Belfast government. This led to bitter resentment, and eventually to the violence that erupted in 1969. It is unlikely that Collins would have ignored the Catholic people in Ulster. He was the one man who was forceful enough to have confronted James Craig and demanded better treatment for the Catholics.

Michael Collins died at a moment when Ireland had most need of him. He was a strong leader, and the country needed strong leadership just then. He had also proved himself an expert in the area of finance, which Ireland also desperately needed. He had a vision of the Ireland he wished to create. With his death, that vision disappeared.

Today, Michael Collins lies in Glasnevin Cemetery in Dublin with his great heroes of the past – heroes who had once ignited a passion for freedom for Ireland in a young boy. When he dreamed of fighting for that freedom as his heroes had, he could never have imagined that, one day, he would lie at peace in the earth with them, regarded as the greatest Irish hero of them all.